Si King & Dave Myers

THE HAIRY
DIETERS

GO VEGGIE

Si King & Dave Myers

THE HAIRY DIETERS

GO VEGGIE

We'd like to dedicate this book to Jinny Johnson, with love and thanks for all the behind-the-scenes support over the years.

First published in Great Britain in 2017 by
Weidenfeld & Nicolson, an imprint of the Orion Publishing Group Ltd
Carmelite House
50 Victoria Embankment
London EC4Y 0DZ
An Hachette UK Company

10 9 8 7 6 5 4 3 2 1

A CIP catalogue record for this book is available from the
British Library.

ISBN: 978 1 4091 7187 4

Printed and bound in Germany

The Orion Publishing Group's policy is to use papers that are natural,
renewable and recyclable and made from wood grown in sustainable
forests. The logging and manufacturing processes are expected to
conform to the environmental regulations of the country of origin.

www.orionbooks.co.uk

Every effort has been made to ensure that the information in this book
is accurate. The information will be relevant to the majority of people
but may not be applicable in each individual case, so it is advised that
professional medical advice is obtained for specific health matters. Neither
the publisher, authors or Optomen accept any legal responsibility for any
personal injury or other damage or loss arising from the use or misuse of
the information in this book. Anyone making a change in their diet should
consult their GP, especially if pregnant, infirm, elderly or under 16.

Food director: Catherine Phipps

Photographer: Andrew Hayes-Watkins

Food stylists: Lisa Harrison,
Anna Burges-Lumsden

Design and art direction: Abi Hartshorne

Project editor: Jinny Johnson

Prop stylist: Sarah Birks

Food stylists' assistant: Lou Kenny

Proofreader: Elise See-Tai

Indexer: Vicki Robinson

Nutritional analysis calculated by:
Fiona Hunter, Bsc (Hons) Nutrition, Dip
Dietetics

CONTENTS

SI AND DAVE GO VEGGIE!

Hey folks – would you believe that we, the Hairy Bikers, well-known lovers of Sunday roasts and meat feasts, are going veggie? Well, at least for some of the time. We know this latest book will come as a big surprise to you. You're used to us as lads who love our meat, and for years we've been busy sharing our recipes for chicken pies, lamb curries and meaty casseroles.

We still love all that – it's part of who we are – but we also know that if you ignore the veggies you're missing out big time. As cooks, we've always appreciated our veg and they're a hugely important part of our cooking. And lately, without really thinking about it, we've been eating less meat. We're not giving it up altogether, but the more we learn about cooking great food, the more we enjoy making use of all the amazing produce that's on offer and creating dishes where vegetables, pulses and other plant foods are the stars of the show. This also fits well with our desire to keep eating healthily and maintain our weight loss.

For this book, we've taken great delight in coming up with dishes that are just as tasty, hearty and satisfying as ever – but without meat. Cut the calories but never the flavour is always our mantra. We're loving this latest exciting step along the way in our culinary adventure and we hope you come with us and enjoy these recipes as much as we do.

THIS IS HOW IT HAPPENED

Last summer, after our holidays, we got together over a few beers to catch up and plan our next projects. Being us, the conversation revolved around food – the ingredients we'd used, the dishes we'd discovered, what we'd enjoyed cooking for family and friends – and we found that we'd been eating very little meat. It seemed to be a natural next step for both of us.

We got really excited about digging deeper into the world of vegetarian cooking. This way of eating fits in so well with the healthy lifestyle we've both adopted in recent years so the plan was obvious – we had to do a vegetarian Hairy Dieters book. There's so much advice now on healthy eating – some of it very confusing – but generally the sensible thing is to eat a diet rich in vegetables, wholegrains and pulses. There's no need for weird ingredients and mysterious potions, just good, tasty food. A veggie diet is also low in saturated fat and high in fibre, which is exactly what the doctor ordered. And because vegetables are lower in calories than meat it's easy to lose weight. You can even have bigger helpings – as long as you don't OD on the cheese, of course.

We did suspect that however much we love our veg we would miss meat – the burgers, the pies, the hotpots. So we came up with our super-tempting 'We Miss Meat' chapter packed with veggie versions of some of our meaty favourites – shepherd's pie, meatballs, lasagne and loads more. There's even toad in the hole, made with our vegetarian sausages, and it's dead good we promise you.

EAT LESS MEAT, SHED A BIT OF WEIGHT

We're not saying we're giving up meat, chicken and fish completely – we enjoy them too much for that. We're just reducing our intake for the good of our waistlines and our health. We might have a meat or fish meal a few times a week, instead of every day. Try eating like this for a while and you'll see a difference in your shopping bills too.

So whether you're a proper full-time vegetarian or just want to eat more healthily and shed a bit of timber, you'll find plenty in this book for you. And you don't have to change to a totally veggie diet overnight. Just start having some meat-free days and see how you go. It's good cooking, good fun and good for you – and the planet.

To help you get started, we've suggested a week's worth of vegetarian menus at the back of this book.

SO WHAT'S IT ALL ABOUT?

When we started working on these recipes, we had a good chat with Fiona, our trusty nutritionist. She helped us clear up some of our worries and answered the questions we all might be too shy to ask. Here goes:

Si: Is a vegetarian diet a good way to eat?

Fiona: Absolutely – there are lots of studies showing that a vegetarian diet can be a very healthy way to eat. In fact, nutritionists are urging us all to eat less meat and more plant-based foods.

Dave: Obviously vegetarians eat veg but can you tell us more?

Fiona: What they don't eat is any fish or meat – this includes chicken! There's nothing that makes vegetarians more furious than people who claim to be vegetarian but still eat chicken or fish.

What vegetarians do eat is all types of fruit and veg, cereals and grains (rice, pasta, potatoes, quinoa, barley, polenta and so on), beans and pulses, nuts and seeds, foods made from soya beans (such as tofu and tempeh), quorn and TVP (textured veg protein).

Most vegetarians also eat dairy foods such as yoghurt, milk, butter, cheese – but see the note on cheese on page 10 – and eggs, although most prefer to have free-range eggs.

You can make veggie versions of your favourite dishes, such as spaghetti Bolognese, chilli, lasagne, burgers, curries and so on, using foods such as beans, mushrooms and tofu as well as vegetables. There are endless possibilities.

Si: What's the difference between vegetarian and vegan?

Fiona: Vegans do not eat animal products in any form, so they avoid dairy foods, eggs and honey as well as meat and fish. They seek to avoid all forms of exploitation of and cruelty to animals for food, clothing and other purposes. They also avoid using products that have been tested on animals.

Dave: What's so healthy about a veggie diet?

Fiona: A diet rich in vegetables is usually lower in saturated fat (the bad sort that clogs your arteries) and higher in fibre (better for your digestive system).

Fruit, vegetables and other plant-based foods are rich in phytochemicals, and a growing body of studies shows that phytochemicals are the magic bullets that protect against many of the conditions associated with ageing. These include some types of cancer, heart disease, dementia, cataracts and age-related macular degeneration, which is the major cause of loss of vision in the western world.

Si: Will I lose weight on a vegetarian diet?

Fiona: It depends on what and how much you eat. Foods such as cheese, nuts and avocados are high in fat, which also means they are high in calories, so it's best to enjoy these foods in moderation. But in general, vegetables are lower in calories than meat, and vegetarian diets are more filling, which can be very helpful when you want to lose weight.

The recipes in this book are all carefully calorie counted and low in fat and sugar, so you'll find it easy to choose dishes that keep you satisfied while losing weight.

Dave: Is it safe for children to go veggie?

Fiona: Yes, it is. A vegetarian diet can provide all the nutrients a child needs to grow and be healthy. A vegan diet can be more difficult, so if you do want to raise your children on a vegan diet it's important to do plenty of research on how to make sure their meals are balanced and healthy. There's lots of information available from the Vegetarian Society and the Vegan Society websites.

Si: How do I make sure I'm getting enough protein?

Fiona: Many new vegetarians are concerned about this but it's really not a problem for two reasons. First, we all tend to eat more protein than we need anyway; second, there are lots of vegetarian foods that are rich in protein, such as nuts, seeds, beans, lentils, eggs and dairy foods.

It used to be said that vegetarian sources of protein were not complete (that is, didn't contain the full complement of essential amino acids) and vegetarians should eat 'complementary proteins' – two different sources of protein at the same meal to provide a 'complete' protein. Experts no longer believe that this is necessary, provided you are eating a good variety of protein foods.

Dave: And what about iron? Don't we need red meat for that?

Fiona: It's true that red meat is the best source of iron, but there are lots of vegetarian foods that also provide iron (see list below). However, iron is one of the nutrients that you must give special consideration to when you stop eating meat – particularly if you have increased requirements for iron (for example, women who have heavy periods).

Iron from vegetarian foods is not as easily absorbed by the body as iron in meat, but there are things you can do to help your body absorb it more easily. Eating foods rich in vitamin C along with food containing iron will improve absorption. For instance, if you have a glass of fruit juice with your breakfast cereal in the morning you will absorb more iron from the cereal.

The following are all good sources of iron for vegetarians:

- Pulses, such as lentils, beans and chickpeas
- Green vegetables – kale, cabbage and broccoli
- Almonds and other nuts
- Wholegrain breakfast cereals and bread
- Tofu
- Dried fruit, such as apricots and dates

Si: Ahem – if I eat beans will I fart a lot?

Fiona: High-fibre foods, such as chickpeas and other pulses, can make you fart and feel bloated – if you are not used to eating them. The good news is that if you introduce them into your diet gradually, eating small amounts to start with, your digestive system will adapt.

Dave: Do I need vitamin supplements if I go veggie?

Fiona: Not necessarily. But if your diet isn't healthy or balanced or if you have a very small or poor appetite, a multi-vitamin and mineral supplement might be a good idea, whether you're vegetarian or not. Certain groups might also benefit from a supplement:

- Women with heavy periods – an iron supplement may be a good idea
- Women who are planning to become pregnant should take a folate supplement
- The elderly and people who don't expose their skin to the sun should take a vitamin D supplement, but check with your pharmacist as some vitamin D supplements aren't suitable for vegetarians
- Vegans should take vitamin B12
- All vegetarians might consider taking an omega-3 supplement – see page 14 for more info

Si: Cheese is fine isn't it? Are there any sorts of cheese vegetarians shouldn't eat?

Fiona: Some cheeses, such as Parmesan, are not suitable for vegetarians because they are made with rennet, which comes from the inside of a calf's stomach. There are plenty of cheeses made with non-animal rennet so check the label to be sure that the cheese is suitable for vegetarians. To replace Parmesan you can buy a Parmesan-style hard cheese.

Dave: What other foods should I avoid?

Fiona: Obviously vegetarians avoid things like meat stock cubes and fish sauce, but there are other less obvious items, such as Worcestershire sauce and gelatine that contain animal products. Some yoghurt contains gelatine, many crisps contain whey, which may be derived from rennet. The red food colouring cochineal is made from crushed insects. Margarine may contain animal fats, fish oils and gelatine. If you're not going totally veggie you might not be worried by all this, but it's good to be aware.

To be sure, always look for a V logo on the packet. The Vegetarian Society produces a really helpful fact sheet with a list of ingredients and products that are not suitable for vegetarians.

Si: Does going veggie cost more?

Fiona: Not at all. Generally, vegetables and other plant-based foods, such as beans, are cheaper than meat and fish.

Dave: What about meat substitutes like quorn, and soya products, such as tofu and tempeh? Are they OK? We both really like tofu.

Fiona: Yes, they're good sources of protein. Quorn has a very similar texture to meat, which some vegetarians find off-putting but others appreciate. Tofu and tempeh are quite bland on their own but can be delicious when marinated with flavourings, such as ginger, soy and chilli. If you like these foods, eat them, but they're not a vital part of a vegetarian diet.

Si: Can you eat bigger helpings of vegetarian food?

Fiona: It depends on the ingredients you're using. Vegetables are low in calories but if you team them with lots of cheese, nuts and oils they can become very calorific. Eat plenty of vegetables and pulses but go easy on the cheese and nuts and you'll be fine.

Dave: Does a vegetarian diet help prevent conditions such as diabetes and high blood pressure?

Fiona: There's plenty of research showing that people who eat a healthy vegetarian diet are less likely to be overweight and have a lower risk of heart disease, high blood pressure, certain types of cancer and diabetes.

Si: Will I get enough good fats on a veggie diet?

Fiona: Nuts, seeds, avocados and vegetable oils all contain good fats so you'll be getting plenty of healthy unsaturated fat. The type of fat that you might not get enough of is the long chain omega-3 fats, which are found in oily fish like salmon. You can buy eggs containing omega-3 fats (produced by hens fed on a diet rich in omega-3s) so this is a good option if you eat eggs. Some foods, such as rapeseed oil, walnuts and linseed, contain omega-3 fats, but they have a different chemical structure to the omega-3s found in fish. If you are particularly concerned there are vegetarian omega-3 supplements (made from algae).

Dave: Is it better to choose low-fat products? Or full-fat? Can we have a bit of butter?

Fiona: This depends on the rest of your diet. Butter is a saturated fat (the sort that clogs your coronary arteries) and so are cheese and other dairy products. On the other hand, butter is natural and if you're not having a lot of saturated fat elsewhere in your diet you can probably get away with eating it.

The golden rule is whatever you choose, eat it in moderation, because all forms of fat – good or bad – contain lots of calories and most of us would probably benefit from eating eat fewer calories. Low-fat foods, such as low-fat yoghurt, half-fat crème fraiche and reduced-fat cheese and coconut milk, are very useful ingredients for keeping the calories down.

Si: And what about alcohol?

Fiona: Animal-derived ingredients are used in the making of many types of cider, beer and wine, but there are brands that do not contain any animal substances. If you're going strictly veggie, look for organic wines and for beverages approved by the Vegetarian Society. Most spirits do not contain animal substances, but they're high in calories so it's best not to overindulge.

A FEW LITTLE NOTES FROM US

We've given calorie counts for all our dishes. Be sure to follow the recipes carefully so you don't change the totals. The calorie counts do not include optional ingredients. Weigh ingredients and use proper spoons and a measuring jug. We always say how many people a recipe serves, so you don't eat more than your share. With these recipes you know exactly where you stand.

We mention spray oil in quite a few recipes, as this is an easy way of reducing the amount of oil you use. Buy the most natural kind you can find and spritz it lightly. If you don't want to use spray oil, just brush on a small amount of oil with a pastry brush. Or buy a plant spray bottle and fill it with the oil of your choice.

The recipes in this book generally include lower-fat ingredients, such as half-fat crème fraiche, semi-skimmed milk and reduced-fat cheese and coconut milk, to keep the calories down. Occasionally we suggest using whole milk where it makes a real difference to a dish

If you're going totally veggie, check that the ingredients you're using are suitable. Buy vegetarian cheese, for example, and organic wines. Look for items approved by the Vegetarian Society.

Peel onions, garlic and all other vegetables and fruit unless otherwise specified.

Use free-range eggs, as fresh as possible, whenever you can. Whatever you're cooking, it always pays to buy the best and freshest seasonal ingredients you can afford. We reckon that 95 per cent of good cooking is good shopping – great ingredients need less fussing about with.

It's useful to have home-made stock in your freezer – have a look at our recipes for vegetarian stocks on pages 180–181. Otherwise, use cubes, bouillon powder or stockpots or the fresh stocks available in many supermarkets now.

BRUNCH

AVOCADO ON TOAST

CREAMED SPINACH WITH EGGS

MEDITERRANEAN BIKER BRUNCH

PUMPKIN PANCAKES WITH APPLE COMPOTE

SMOKED TOFU AND VEGETABLE HASH

VEGETABLE JUICE BLOODY MARY

AVOCADO ON TOAST

Avo on toast is not just for skinny blondes! Kingy's been loving it for years and eating it with pride – often with a poached egg on top. In this recipe, the avocado's poshed up with some extra flavours to make it really special. Za'atar is a beautifully fragrant Middle Eastern spice. It's available in lots of supermarkets now, but if you don't have any, it's fine to leave it out.

4 slices of
sourdough bread

2 avocados

juice of ½ lemon

16 cherry tomatoes,
quartered

1 tsp grated lemon zest

1 tsp olive oil

a few dashes of mild
vinegar (brown rice
vinegar is good)

a few dashes of hot sauce

small bunch of coriander
or parsley

pinches of
smoked paprika

pinches of za'atar
(optional)

½ tsp sesame seeds

sea salt and black pepper

Toast the sourdough. Roughly mash the avocados in a bowl with a generous pinch of salt and the lemon juice. Spread this over the toasted sourdough.

Toss the cherry tomatoes with the lemon zest, olive oil, vinegar and hot sauce. Tear the coriander or parsley leaves and mix them with the tomatoes. Season them with salt and pepper, then divide them between the avocado-covered toast.

Sprinkle with pinches of paprika, za'atar, if using, and sesame seeds and serve immediately.

Serves 4 | 249 calories per serving; 488 calories per serving with rosti
Prep: 15 minutes | Cooking time: 20–25 minutes

CREAMED SPINACH WITH EGGS

Mmmm – this tastes rich and luxurious and even though it contains cream and cheese it still comes in at a reasonable calorie count. A belter of a brunch dish, it's a sort of healthier version of eggs Florentine, a dish we've loved for years. It also makes a good quick supper – especially when served with our root vegetable rosti (see page 175).

10g butter
1 onion, finely chopped
¼ tsp ground turmeric
¼ tsp ground cumin
pinch each of nutmeg and cinnamon
300g spinach, washed and roughly chopped
150ml single cream
50g reduced-fat Cheddar cheese, grated
4 eggs
sea salt and black pepper

Melt the butter in a large frying pan and add the onion with a pinch of salt. Cook the onion over a gentle heat until it's soft and translucent. Sprinkle in the spices with some freshly ground black pepper and stir to coat the onion.

Add the spinach and stir, pushing the leaves down into the pan until they have wilted. Turn up the heat slightly and continue to cook and stir until any liquid from the spinach has evaporated.

Pour in the single cream and keep stirring until the cream has reduced – the spinach should be well broken down and creamy, but not wet. Add half the grated cheese and stir it through until it has melted.

Meanwhile, bring a saucepan of water to the boil. Lower the eggs gently into the water and cook them for 6 minutes. Remove the eggs from the pan and put them in a bowl of cold water to stop the cooking process.

Carefully peel the eggs and cut them in half lengthways. Push the eggs into the spinach, yolk-side up, then sprinkle over the rest of the cheese. Cover and cook until the eggs are warmed through and the cheese has melted. You can put the pan under a grill instead if you prefer the cheese to brown. Serve at once – with some rosti (see page 175) if you fancy.

MEDITERRANEAN BIKER BRUNCH

Piperade, the popular Basque dish, was our inspiration for this recipe. We've fiddled about a bit, added some fennel and other extra flavours and come up with what we think is a real winner – some sunshine on a plate whenever you need it. You can make the veg in advance if you like, then reheat it and add the eggs.

10ml olive oil

1 red and 1 green pepper, deseeded and cut into strips

1 fennel bulb, trimmed and cut into thin wedges

1 tsp fennel seeds

½ tsp coriander seeds

½ tsp chilli flakes

1 piece of thinly pared orange zest

400g can of tomatoes, or fresh equivalent

4 eggs

1 tsp white wine vinegar

a few basil leaves, shredded, to serve

sea salt and black pepper

Heat the olive oil in a large frying pan with a lid. Add the peppers and fennel with a splash of water, cover the pan and cook for 10–15 minutes, stirring regularly.

Lightly crush the fennel seeds and coriander seeds. Add them to the pan with the chilli flakes, orange zest and a generous amount of salt and pepper, then add the tomatoes and stir. Add another splash of water and simmer gently until the peppers and fennel are tender and the sauce is nicely reduced.

To poach the eggs, half fill a saucepan with water, and add the vinegar. Bring the water to the boil, then carefully lower the eggs (still in their shells) into the water and leave them for exactly 20 seconds. Remove the eggs from the water. Turn the heat down so the water is barely simmering. Carefully crack each egg into the water and cook them for 3 minutes. Once the eggs are cooked they will rise to the surface. Remove the eggs from the pan and put them on some kitchen paper to drain before serving.

Remove the piece of orange zest, then serve the veg topped with the eggs and a few basil leaves.

PUMPKIN PANCAKES
WITH APPLE COMPOTE

These are a really great take on a pancake and you can use canned unsweetened pumpkin to make things quick and easy. Serve the pancakes with apple compote and some crème fraiche or low-fat yoghurt or just drizzle a little maple syrup over them. Epic!

150g unsweetened pumpkin purée (from a can)
1 egg, separated
225ml milk
25g soft light brown sugar
125g wholemeal or spelt flour
1 tsp baking powder
1 tsp ground cinnamon
grating of nutmeg
pinch of salt
low-cal oil spray

Apple compote

3 eating apples (such as Cox), diced
juice of ½ lemon
½ tsp ground cinnamon
pinch of cloves
25ml maple syrup or soft light brown sugar

To serve (optional)

half-fat crème fraiche or low-fat set yoghurt

First make the apple compote. Put the apples in a small saucepan and add the lemon juice, cinnamon, cloves and maple syrup or sugar. Pour over 100ml of water, then cook gently until the apples are softened and fluffy. Add a little more water if necessary. Set the compote aside and keep it warm.

For the pancakes, mix the pumpkin purée, egg yolk, milk and sugar in a bowl until smooth. Mix the flour, baking powder and spices together in a separate bowl and add a pinch of salt, then whisk these dry ingredients into the pumpkin mixture. In another bowl, whisk the egg white until stiff. Carefully fold it into the pancake batter, mixing lightly but thoroughly until no streaks of egg white remain.

Spray a large frying pan with low-cal oil and place it over a medium heat. When the pan is hot, dollop on heaped tablespoons of the batter, spreading them out a little. You should be able to cook 4 pancakes at a time. Wait until bubbles appear on each pancake and they look set around the edges, then flip them over. Cook for another couple of minutes, then remove the pancakes from the pan and keep them warm. Continue until you have used up all the batter, spraying the pan in between each batch.

Serve the pumpkin pancakes with the compote and some crème fraiche or yoghurt if you like.

SMOKED TOFU AND VEGETABLE HASH

Smoked tofu is a wonderful product to tempt the dedicated meat eater. We think of it as vegetarian smoky bacon! Top this fry-up with an egg and you've got a proper feast for a Sunday morning.

1 tbsp olive oil

1 large red onion, finely chopped

2 sweet potatoes, (about 400g peeled weight) diced

200g broccoli, roughly chopped

200g spring greens, shredded

200g smoked tofu, finely diced

1 garlic clove, finely chopped

1 tsp mushroom ketchup

1 tbsp tomato ketchup or purée

200ml vegetable stock or water

4 eggs

1 tsp white wine vinegar (for poaching eggs) or low-cal oil spray (for frying)

sea salt

Heat the olive oil in a large frying pan and add the red onion. Cook it over a medium heat until it's translucent, softened and starting to brown.

Meanwhile, bring a large saucepan of water to the boil. Add salt, then the diced sweet potatoes. Bring the water back to the boil, then simmer the sweet potatoes for 2 minutes. Add the broccoli and spring greens and cook for another 2 minutes. Drain the vegetables thoroughly.

Add the sweet potato, broccoli, spring greens, smoked tofu and garlic to the frying pan with the onion. Whisk the mushroom ketchup and tomato ketchup or purée with the stock or water, then pour this over the vegetables. Cook for 5 minutes, or until most of the liquid has been absorbed, stirring regularly. Pat everything down fairly evenly, turn up the heat a little and allow a crust to form on the bottom. Stir, scraping up any brown bits from the bottom of the pan, then pat the mixture down again, and leave it for another 10 minutes. Stir thoroughly.

While the hash is cooking, poach the eggs (see page 23) or fry them (see page 153). Serve the hash topped with the eggs.

Per 200ml | 50 calories (juice only); 100 calories (with vodka and sherry)
Prep: 10 minutes | Cooking time: 25 minutes

VEGETABLE JUICE BLOODY MARY

You can make a super-healthy vegetable juice and drink it straight or you can add a tot of vodka and make a bloody Mary – known by us as electric soup! Either way you're getting some goodness from the veggies. We find that cooking the veg like this makes the juice taste better and they do say that cooked tomatoes are better for you than raw. Passata and canned tomatoes often have a slightly metallic taste which disappears when they're cooked. Mix all this up and enjoy – cheers!

Juice
1kg tomato passata
2 carrots, finely chopped
1 slice of beetroot, finely chopped
2 celery sticks, finely chopped
1 tbsp mushroom ketchup
50g spinach, roughly chopped
small bunch of parsley, roughly chopped
sea salt and black pepper

Bloody Mary (per person)
plenty of ice cubes
1 measure (or 2!) of vodka
1 tsp sherry
dash of Tabasco sauce
celery stick

Put the passata, carrots, beetroot, celery and mushroom ketchup in a saucepan and cover with 100ml of water. Season with salt and pepper. Bring to the boil, then turn down the heat, cover the pan and leave the veg to simmer for 20 minutes.

Add the spinach and parsley, cover the pan again and simmer for another 5 minutes. Remove the pan from the heat and set the veg aside to cool.

Pour the cooled mixture into a blender and add another 150ml of water. Blitz, then, if you want your juice to be completely smooth, push it through a sieve. Add more water if the juice seems too thick. Chill the juice in the fridge before serving. If the mixture separates, give it a good stir and it will come together again.

To serve as a Bloody Mary, add ice cubes to a highball glass, then add vodka and top up with the juice. Add a teaspoon of sherry, a dash of Tabasco and stir with a stick of celery.

STARTERS AND SNACKS

VEGETARIAN SUSHI

SPRING ROLLS

SUPER SATAY

ONION FLOWER

ARTICHOKE AND LEMON DIP

FETA AND SPINACH CIGARILLOS

ROAST CHICKPEAS

LIL'S ROAST VEGETABLE DIP

CURRIED PUMPKIN FRITTERS
WITH CORIANDER DIPPING SAUCE

SOCCA AND SALSA

Makes 24 rolls | 44 calories per roll (avocado); 27 calories per roll (cucumber and radish); 28 calories per roll (mushroom) | Prep: 30 minutes (plus rice standing time)
Cooking time: up to 15 minutes

VEGETARIAN SUSHI

Being a pair of dedicated sushi monsters, we find these maki roll-style goodies really hit the spot. All the filling quantities make enough for 24 rolls, but you could reduce the quantities if you want to make a couple of different kinds. We think these make an ideal starter to a veggie meal.

150g sushi rice
2 tbsp sushi vinegar
2 sheets of nori
sea salt

Avocado filling
½ avocado, cut lengthways into thin batons
½ tsp black sesame seeds
sprinkling of chilli powder

Cucumber and radish filling
½ cucumber, deseeded and cut into thin batons
2 radishes, cut into batons
1 tsp rice wine vinegar
pinch of sugar

Mushroom filling
6 shiitake mushrooms
1 tsp oil
1 garlic clove
1 tsp mirin
1 tsp brown rice vinegar

First cook the sushi rice. Rinse the rice in water, changing the water several times until it's clear. Drain the rice thoroughly and leave it to stand for at least 15 minutes.

Put the rice in a saucepan with 175ml of water and a pinch of salt. Cover the pan and bring the water to the boil, then turn down the heat and simmer for 5 minutes. Turn off the heat and leave the rice to stand for 10–15 minutes until all the water is absorbed.

Transfer the rice to a shallow baking dish or tray and cool it down as quickly as possible. This is traditionally done by fanning it, so use a fan if you have one. If not, a piece of cardboard will do fine. When the rice is almost cool, pour the sushi vinegar over it and mix thoroughly. You can use the rice once it is at room temperature.

To make the avocado filling or the cucumber and radish filling, mix the ingredients together.

To make the mushroom filling, trim off the stems of the mushrooms and slice them finely. Heat the oil in a small frying pan and add the mushrooms. Cook until they have given out their liquid and the pan is dry, then add the garlic. Cook for a further couple of minutes, then pour over the mirin and brown rice vinegar. Season with salt.

To serve
soy sauce
wasabi paste
sushi ginger

To make the sushi, lie half a sheet of nori across the bottom of a sushi mat, rough-side up, shiny-side down. Spread a quarter of the rice over the nori, as evenly as you can, leaving a 1cm edge along the top. Arrange your chosen filling in a line across the middle of rice.

Using the mat, start rolling up the sushi as tightly as you can, until the filling is entirely encased. Take a very sharp knife and cut the roll in half, then cut each half into 3 equal pieces, wiping the knife in between each cut. Repeat with the remaining nori.

Serve with soy sauce, wasabi paste and sushi ginger if you like.

SPRING ROLLS

These might sound a bit fiddly but you soon get the hang of rolling up the little beauties and they make a really tasty starter. If you would prefer vegan rolls, just use a paste of water and plain flour instead of beaten egg for brushing. The rolls should still hold together well.

12 spring roll wrappers OR 15cm squares of filo pastry
1 egg, beaten
sesame oil
soy sauce, to serve

Filling
2 medium carrots, cut into thin batons (discard the cores)
1 large courgette, shredded
4 spring onions, finely chopped
100g Chinese cabbage, shredded
20g fresh root ginger, finely chopped
1 tsp Chinese five-spice powder
1 tbsp soy sauce
1 tsp sesame seeds
dash of sesame oil

Preheat the oven to 200°C/Fan 180°C/Gas 6. Put all the filling ingredients into a bowl and mix them together thoroughly.

To assemble the spring rolls, take a wrapper and place it on your work surface so one of the points faces downwards (like a diamond).

Take a large heaped tablespoon of the filling (30–35g) and place it in a thick line across the spring roll wrapper, between a third and half way up. Brush all the exposed pastry with beaten egg. Fold the bottom corner over the filling, pushing it down gently so it follows the contours of the filling. Brush again with beaten egg, then fold in the 2 sides to enclose the filling, then roll up. Repeat to make the rest of the spring rolls and place them all on a baking tray.

If using filo to make your spring rolls, use 2 squares to make each roll.

Add a few drops of sesame oil to the remaining beaten egg and brush this liberally over the spring rolls. Bake them in the preheated oven for about 20 minutes until they're crisp and golden brown. Serve with some extra soy sauce for dipping.

SUPER SATAY

Tempeh and tofu make great satay. They're both soya products and are a useful source of protein for vegetarians. Tempeh is higher in calories but is less processed than tofu and contains more fibre. Neither has much taste but they absorb other flavours so work well with this marinade and peanut sauce. Don't forget to soak your bamboo skewers for half an hour so they don't burn.

400g tempeh or tofu
sesame oil, to serve

Marinade
1 lemongrass stem, white part only, chopped
30g fresh root ginger, roughly chopped
3 garlic cloves, chopped
1 tsp chilli flakes
zest and juice of 1 lime
1 tsp honey or palm sugar
1 tbsp soy sauce
1 tbsp mild curry powder
a few drops of sesame oil

Peanut sauce
2 tbsp peanut butter
50ml reduced-calorie coconut milk
juice of ½ lemon
1 tsp maple syrup
1 tsp hot sauce, such as sriracha
1 tbsp soy sauce
1 garlic clove, crushed
sea salt and black pepper

Put the marinade ingredients into a blender or food processor and blitz them to a smooth paste. Add a little water if necessary.

Cut the tempeh or tofu into large cubes, put them in a bowl and pour over the marinade ingredients. Turn the tempeh or tofu over very gently so you don't break it up, making sure it is completely covered with the marinade. Leave for as long as you can – at least half an hour.

Make the peanut sauce. Whisk all the ingredients together and season with salt and pepper. Set aside.

When you are ready to cook the tempeh or tofu, arrange the cubes on soaked bamboo skewers. Heat a griddle pan and when it's too hot to hold your hand over comfortably, add the skewers, well spread out. Grill each side of the cubes until they're nicely browned and charred.

Drizzle the tempeh or tofu with a little sesame oil and serve immediately. A little cucumber salad (see page 174) scattered with some sesame seeds is a good accompaniment.

ONION FLOWER

Who would have guessed you could elevate the humble onion to the dizzy heights of a blooming flower? The onion opens out beautifully when baked and wouldn't go amiss on Carmen Miranda's hat! We like this American-style cocktail sauce with it, but a blue cheese dip would also be good.

1 large Spanish onion
15g butter, melted
15g fine breadcrumbs
15g vegetarian Parmesan-style hard cheese, grated
1 tbsp finely chopped parsley
grated zest of ½ lime
½ tsp smoked paprika
sea salt and black pepper

Dipping sauce
2 tbsp reduced-fat mayonnaise
2 tbsp half-fat crème fraiche
1 tbsp tomato ketchup
1 tbsp horseradish sauce
juice of 1 lime
dash of Tabasco sauce

Line a roasting tin with foil, making sure it overlaps the sides so that you can wrap up the onion.

Peel the onion. Trim the top and any straggly bits from the root, but leave the root intact. Cut the onion into 16 wedges, almost down to the root, making sure the wedges are still attached to the base. Soak the onion in a bowl of iced water for half an hour. Preheat the oven to 200°C/Fan 180°C/Gas 6.

Drain the onion thoroughly and place it in the roasting tin. Press the wedges down, opening them up into their individual slices, then season well with salt and pepper. Bring the sides of the foil up around the onion and seal. Bake the onion in the oven for about 20 minutes, until just tender.

Remove the onion from the oven and open up the foil parcel. Brush the onion with the melted butter. Mix together the breadcrumbs, cheese, parsley, lime zest and paprika, then sprinkle this mixture over the onion.

Leave the onion uncovered, put it back in the oven and bake for another 25–30 minutes until crisp and brown on the tips.

Mix together the sauce ingredients and season with salt and pepper. Serve it with the onion so everyone can pull out onion 'petals' and dip them in the sauce.

ARTICHOKE AND LEMON DIP

Those roasted artichokes in oil you can buy from the deli counter or in jars are just right for this – better than the ones in brine – but you do have to drain and rinse them thoroughly to keep the cal count down. You still get a nice creamy dip that makes a great snack with some cucumber, celery and other raw veg. This is a life-saver for those snack-attack moments.

200g roasted artichokes
grated zest of 1 lemon
juice of ½ lemon
1 garlic clove, crushed
small bunch of basil, leaves only
15g vegetarian Parmesan-style hard cheese, grated
150g half-fat crème fraiche
sea salt and black pepper

Drain the roasted artichokes and rinse them thoroughly as the oil will add calories.

Put the artichokes in a food processor with the remaining ingredients and season well with salt and pepper. Blitz until the mixture is fairly smooth – it's good to keep a little texture, but you don't want the dip to be lumpy or fibrous. You may need to push the mixture down with a spatula a couple of times.

Cover and store the dip in the fridge until needed. It will keep well for a couple of days.

FETA AND SPINACH CIGARILLOS

Dieting or not, we all need a snack sometimes. These are veggie but fill the bill for everyone.

low-cal oil spray
100g reduced-fat feta
150g frozen spinach, defrosted
2 tbsp finely chopped coriander
1 tsp dried mint
zest of ½ lemon
½ tsp smoked paprika
pinch of cayenne
4 large sheets of filo pastry
sea salt and black pepper

Preheat the oven to 180°C/Fan 160°C/Gas 4. Spray a baking tray with low-cal oil.

Crumble the feta into a bowl. Squeeze out as much water as you can from the spinach and chop it finely, then add it to the bowl with the feta. Add the herbs, lemon zest and spices, then season with salt and pepper, and mix thoroughly.

Cut the filo sheets into quarters, so you have 16 squares or rectangles. The size you end up with will depend on the original size of the filo – ours were 16cm x 19cm. Take one of your filo quarters and lay it short-side towards you, if rectangular. Give it a couple of squirts of low-cal oil spray and brush the oil lightly over the sheet, being careful not to tear it.

Take a teaspoon of the filling and roll it into a thin log, 2cm shorter than the short side of your filo sheet. Lie this along the bottom of the filo sheet, leaving a 2cm border, then tightly roll up the filo, folding in the sides once the filling is completely enclosed.

Put the rolled sheet on to the prepared baking tray and continue until you have 16 cigarillos. Spray them once more with the low-cal oil and bake in the oven for 20 minutes until they're crisp and golden brown. You can serve these straight from the oven but they are also good at room temperature.

ROAST CHICKPEAS

These make a cracking good snack and you can add chilli, paprika or whatever spice you fancy.

400g can of chickpeas,
drained and rinsed
1 tbsp olive oil
zest of 1 lemon
½ tsp rosemary
1 tsp sumac
sea salt and black pepper

Preheat the oven to 200°C/Fan 180°C/Gas 6. Dry the chickpeas by wrapping them in a tea towel, or by gently blotting them with kitchen paper, then put them in a bowl. Drizzle over the olive oil, then add the lemon zest and a generous amount of salt and black pepper.

Spread the chickpeas over a baking tray, then roast them in the oven for 25–30 minutes. Check them regularly and give the tray a shake so the chickpeas roast evenly. The chickpeas are done when they are nicely browned and crisp on the outside, but still soft on the inside. Transfer the chickpeas to a bowl, then add the rosemary and sumac and stir. Great hot or cold.

LIL'S ROAST VEGETABLE DIP

Lil, Dave's wife, makes this lush dip, which is called zacusca in Romania and is an Eastern European classic. We've adapted it slightly, reducing the amount of oil to cut the calories and adding paprika instead of fresh pimentos and we think you're going to love it. Do use fresh tomatoes – they really make a difference here. Serve this dip with raw veg or the socca on page 49.

1 aubergine
1 red pepper, deseeded and cut in half
1 tbsp olive oil
1 onion, finely chopped
150g ripe tomatoes
2 garlic cloves, finely grated or crushed
1 tsp sweet smoked paprika
¼ tsp hot smoked paprika
1 bay leaf
1 piece of thinly pared lemon zest (optional)
sea salt and black or white pepper

Preheat the oven to 220°C/Fan 200°C/Gas 7. Make a few holes in the aubergine and place it on a baking tray with the red pepper. Roast the aubergine and pepper in the preheated oven for 35–40 minutes, turning the aubergine over once or twice, until the skin is blackened. Remove them from the oven. Cut the aubergine in half and leave it to drain for a few minutes. Put the red pepper halves in a bowl and cover with a plate or cling film, then when they're cool enough to handle, peel off the skin.

Meanwhile, heat the oil in a saucepan. Add the onion with a splash of water, then cover the pan and cook the onion over a low heat for about 10 minutes until soft, stirring regularly.

To peel the tomatoes, score a cross in the base of each one. Put them in a bowl, pour over freshly boiled water and count to 10, then drain. The skin will peel off very easily. Chop them finely.

Add the garlic and paprikas to the onion in the pan and cook for another couple of minutes. Finely chop the aubergine and red pepper and add them to the onions along with the tomatoes. Season with salt and plenty of pepper. Tuck in a bay leaf and lemon zest, if using, then simmer, covered, for half an hour. Uncover and continue to cook, stirring regularly, until thick.

This is good as it is but if you want a smooth dip, purée it in a blender or food processor – take out the bay leaf and lemon zest first. Leave the dip to cool down and serve at room temperature.

CURRIED PUMPKIN FRITTERS
WITH CORIANDER DIPPING SAUCE

We do love a fritter and these are extra good – nice and crispy on the outside and soft and tasty within. If you want to add an extra spicy kick you could sprinkle in some chopped chilli or chilli flakes. Chickpea flour, also known as gram flour, is great for fritters and it's gluten free if that's a concern for you. It's available in supermarkets as well as in Indian grocery stores.

50g chickpea (gram) flour
or plain flour
1 tsp baking powder
1 tsp mild curry powder
1 egg
30ml milk or water
1 small onion,
finely chopped
200g pumpkin or squash,
coarsely grated
1 garlic clove, grated
15g fresh root ginger,
peeled and grated
1 tbsp finely chopped
coriander
1 tsp dried mint
low-cal oil spray or 1 tsp
vegetable oil
sea salt and black pepper

Coriander dipping sauce
small bunch of fresh
coriander
juice of ½ lemon
pinch of sugar
100ml low-fat yoghurt

Put the flour into a bowl, add the baking powder, curry powder and a pinch of salt and whisk together to combine. Break in the egg and mix until you have a very thick paste, then gradually add the milk or water to make a smooth batter.

Add the onion, pumpkin or squash, garlic, ginger, coriander and mint and stir to combine.

Cover the base of a frying pan with a few spritzes of oil spray or add a teaspoon of oil, then heat the pan. Dollop in heaped dessertspoonfuls of the batter – you should be able to fit 4. Flatten the fritters out as much as you can – they will puff up slightly – and cook for 3–4 minutes on each side until crisp and brown. Remove the fritters from the pan and keep them warm while you cook the rest in the same way.

For the sauce, blitz the coriander, lemon juice and sugar in a blender with plenty of seasoning and a splash of water if necessary – you want the sauce to be fairly smooth. Stir in the yoghurt, then serve the sauce with the fritters.

SOCCA AND SALSA

We have to warn you: these chickpea flour flatbreads – socca, also known as farinata – are addictive! You can leave them plain, just seasoned with salt and pepper, or jazz them up with lots of herbs and caramelised onions as here. Either way you're going to love them – try them with a cold beer once the diet is over! Cut them into wedges or serve whole for people to tear off pieces and enjoy with the tomato salsa below or either of the dips in this chapter.

2 tbsp olive oil

2 red onions, sliced into thin wedges

150g chickpea (gram) flour

1 tsp finely chopped rosemary

low-cal oil spray or olive oil

sea salt and black pepper

Salsa

4 tomatoes, cored and diced

½ small red onion, finely chopped

1 small red chilli, finely chopped

zest of ½ lemon

1 tsp red wine vinegar

1 tsp olive oil

small bunch of basil, finely chopped

Heat a tablespoon of the oil in a frying pan and add the red onions. Fry them over a medium heat for at least 10 minutes until they have softened and started to caramelise. Set aside.

Put the chickpea flour in a bowl with a generous pinch of salt and whisk to remove any lumps. Gradually pour in 250ml of water and continue to whisk until you have a smooth batter with the consistency of thick double cream. Stir in the remaining olive oil and whisk to emulsify. Set the batter aside.

To make the salsa, mix all the ingredients in a bowl and season well with salt and pepper.

You can make 2 large socca in a 25cm non-stick pan, or 4 in a smaller pan. If making 2 large socca, heat the pan and spritz with oil spray or pour a few drops of oil into the pan and rub it over the base with kitchen paper. Pour half the batter into the pan and swirl to cover the base. Sprinkle over half the onions and half the rosemary, then cook over a medium heat for a few minutes until browned and crisping round the edges. Flip the socca over to cook the other side or put the pan under a medium grill to finish the cooking. Transfer it to a board or a large plate and repeat.

If you are cooking 4 socca, split the batter into 4 and proceed as above, using a quarter of the onions and rosemary each time. Cut the socca into wedges or serve whole with the salsa.

SOUPS AND SALADS

MISO SOUP

SPRING VEGGIE BROTH WITH DUMPLINGS

COURGETTE, MINT AND LEMON SOUP

MULLIGATAWNY

VEGETABLE CHOWDER

RED LENTIL AND HARISSA SOUP

VEGGIE SCOTCH BROTH

BEETROOT, FENNEL AND BLUE CHEESE SALAD

GADO GADO SALAD

SMOKED TOFU, AVOCADO AND SPINACH SALAD

GOAT'S CHEESE, PEACH AND RADICCHIO SALAD

JUMBO COUSCOUS SALAD

TOMATO, FETA AND WATERMELON SALAD

MISO SOUP

We do love our miso soup and it's good at any time of day – we sometimes have it for breakfast. This is a version without dashi stock as the regular sort contains bonito flakes so isn't vegetarian. The soup is still proper tasty though, particularly if you use our mushroom stock (see page 180). For the tofu, look for firm not silken, which is too soft for this dish. And if you want a more substantial meal, add some soba noodles to your bowl of goodness.

800ml vegetable or mushroom stock (see p. 180)

4 tbsp miso paste

1 garlic clove, crushed

15g fresh root ginger, grated

soy sauce, to taste

100g shiitake mushrooms, sliced

100g enoki mushrooms (or any other sort)

100g oyster mushrooms, sliced

4 spring onions, diagonally sliced

2–3 heads of Asian greens

a sheet of nori seaweed

100g firm tofu, diced

salt (optional)

To serve (optional)

a few drops of sesame oil

a few drops of chilli oil

100g dried soba noodles

Pour the stock into a large saucepan and add the miso paste, garlic and ginger. Heat the stock gently and keep stirring until the miso paste has completely dissolved into the liquid. Taste, then add a dash of soy sauce and a little salt if necessary. Add all the mushrooms, the spring onions and greens and simmer for 2–3 minutes until they have softened.

Tear the seaweed into pieces and divide them and the tofu between 4 bowls. Taste the broth and add a little more soy to taste, then ladle it over the seaweed and tofu. Add a few drops of sesame oil and/or chilli oil to each bowl if you like.

If you're adding noodles, cook them according to the packet instructions and add them to the bowls.

SPRING VEGGIE BROTH WITH DUMPLINGS

It's well worth making your own stock for this one (see page 181), using the asparagus trimmings and pea pods – why waste all that goodness? The soup is light and fragrant and we've added some little low-fat dumplings which taste naughtier than they are – which has to be a good thing! This does need a bit of planning, as the dumplings should be made the night before serving the soup.

Dumplings

150g ricotta or low-fat quark

25g vegetarian Parmesan-style hard cheese, grated

a few basil leaves, very finely chopped

semolina, for dusting

sea salt and black pepper

Soup

800ml spring vegetable stock (see p. 181)

50g baby new potatoes, scraped and sliced into rounds

50g baby carrots, trimmed and halved lengthways

4 baby leeks or 6 spring onions, shredded

1 sprig of tarragon

1 strip of pared lime zest

200g asparagus, trimmed and cut into lengths

2 small courgettes, sliced into thin rounds

100g peas, either freshly podded or frozen

4 artichoke hearts, sliced (optional)

Make the dumplings the night before. Drain the ricotta or quark and put it in a bowl. Break it up with a fork, add the grated hard cheese and the basil leaves and season well, then mix everything together.

Sprinkle some semolina over a small roasting tin or tray. Wet the palms of your hands and dip them in the semolina – this will stop the dumplings sticking to your hands too much. Form the mixture into 12 small dumplings, dropping them into the semolina as you go. Cover with more semolina, then leave the dumplings to chill in the fridge overnight.

To make the soup, heat the stock in a large saucepan. Add the new potatoes, carrots, leeks or spring onions, tarragon and lime zest, then season with salt. Bring to the boil, then cover the pan and simmer the soup for 10 minutes.

Add the asparagus, courgettes, peas and artichoke hearts, if using, and simmer for a few more minutes until the potatoes and carrots are cooked through and the green vegetables are still fresh and al dente.

Bring a saucepan of water to the boil and add salt. Turn the heat down to a simmer. Shake off any excess semolina from the dumplings and drop them into the water. Cook the dumplings for 4–5 minutes – when they float up to the top they are done.

Basil oil
1 tbsp olive oil
small bunch of basil

Carefully remove the dumplings with a slotted spoon – they will be fragile.

To make the basil oil, whizz the oil and basil together with a tiny amount of water if necessary, then set aside

Serve the soup in shallow bowls, add the dumplings and drizzle the basil oil on top.

COURGETTE, MINT AND LEMON SOUP

Courgette soups are often made with milk or cream and are quite rich, but we've kept ours nice and fresh and simple. If you're a vegan, this is one for you and if not – try it anyway as it's really tasty, super-green and keeps you lean.

1 tbsp olive oil

1 onion, finely chopped

1 potato, finely diced

750g courgettes, coarsely grated

2 garlic cloves, finely chopped

grated zest of 1 lemon

1 tsp dried mint

750ml vegetable stock

100g frozen peas

100g baby spinach

squeeze of lemon juice (optional)

sea salt and black pepper

Heat the olive oil in a large saucepan, add the onion and potato and stir well to coat them in the oil. Add a splash of water, cover the pan and cook the veg gently for about 10 minutes. Add the courgettes, garlic, lemon zest and mint, then cook for another 2 minutes.

Pour in the stock, season with salt and pepper and bring to the boil. Simmer for about 5 minutes, then add the peas and spinach. Cook for another 2 minutes until the spinach has completely wilted and the peas are just tender but still fresh and green looking.

Purée the soup in a blender or with a stick blender, but be careful not to over process it, as you want to keep some flecks of green throughout. Taste and add a squeeze of lemon juice, if using, and more seasoning if you like before serving.

If you want to make your soup a bit more fancy, decorate it with ribbons of courgette and some sprinkles of lemon zest.

MULLIGATAWNY

There are lots of stories about the origins of this wonderful curry-flavoured soup, but it seems that it most likely came from India, and then become a great British favourite. It's usually made with chicken stock and chicken, but our veggie version is just as good. As we've always said – there are no calories in flavour and this soup is certainly not lacking in that department.

1 tsp vegetable oil
1 onion, diced
2 garlic cloves, finely chopped
20g fresh root ginger, finely chopped
1 red chilli, finely chopped
1 carrot, diced
150g butternut squash or sweet potato, diced
1 tbsp curry powder
1 litre vegetable stock
100g basmati rice, well rinsed
200g chickpeas (from a can)
100g frozen peas
1 apple, cored and diced
bunch of fresh coriander, chopped, to serve

Yoghurt and mango dressing
100ml low-fat yoghurt
1 tbsp mango chutney

Heat the oil in a large saucepan. Add the onion and fry it over a medium heat for a few minutes until it's starting to colour. Add the garlic, ginger, chilli, carrot and butternut squash or sweet potato, stir for a minute or so, then sprinkle in the curry powder. Stir to coat all the veg in the curry powder.

Pour in the vegetable stock. Bring the stock to the boil and simmer for about 20 minutes until the vegetables are tender. Whizz the soup a couple of times with a stick blender to break up some of the vegetables or remove about a quarter of the soup and blend it, then pour it back into the pan.

While the vegetables are cooking, cook the rice in plenty of salted water according to the packet instructions. Drain the rice well and refresh it in cold water.

Add the chickpeas, cooked rice, peas and apple to the soup and simmer for 2–3 minutes.

Mix the yoghurt with the mango chutney. Serve the soup sprinkled with plenty of freshly chopped coriander and the yoghurt and chutney on the side for everyone to dollop on to their bowlful.

VEGETABLE CHOWDER

This chowder is real comfort food. It's rich and creamy with a nutty sweetness from the cauliflower but is still surprisingly low in calories. A bowl of this makes a perfect lunch on a chilly day – it's a cuddle in a bowl.

10g butter
1 onion, finely diced
2 celery sticks, diced
3 garlic cloves, finely chopped
150g potato, diced
250g sweet potato, diced
250g cauliflower, cut into very small florets
800ml vegetable stock
2 leeks, sliced
100g frozen sweetcorn
200ml whole milk
sea salt and black pepper

Melt the butter in a large saucepan. Add the onion and celery, then cover the pan and cook them over a low heat for about 10 minutes. Add the garlic and cook for another couple of minutes, then add the potato, sweet potato and cauliflower. Stir everything well, then pour the stock into the pan. Season with salt and pepper, bring the stock to the boil, then turn the heat down and put a lid on the saucepan.

Simmer for about 20 minutes, then add the leeks and sweetcorn. Continue to simmer the soup, covered, for another 10–15 minutes, until the vegetables are starting to collapse, then add the milk and heat through. Mash the soup very slightly and add a little more stock if you need. Taste and adjust the seasoning if necessary before serving.

RED LENTIL AND HARISSA SOUP

Quick to prepare, this soup is made with ingredients that you probably have in your store cupboard and the harissa paste brings a great warm spiciness. It packs a punch of flavour and warms the cockles on a cold day. Gremolata is just a nice little seasoning of garlic, lemon and parsley to add a bit of oomph to the soup.

1 tbsp olive oil

1 large onion, finely chopped

2 garlic cloves, finely chopped

2 tbsp finely chopped coriander stems

1–2 tbsp harissa paste (depending on how much heat you want)

200g red lentils, rinsed

1 litre vegetable stock

400g can of tomatoes

squeeze of lemon (optional)

sea salt and black pepper

Gremolata

zest of 1 lemon

1 garlic clove, finely chopped

coriander leaves, finely chopped

Heat the oil in a large saucepan. Add the onion and cook it over a gentle heat until softened. Add the garlic and cook for another minute, then stir in the coriander stems and the harissa paste.

Add the lentils and stir until they are coated with the paste, then pour over the stock and season with salt and pepper. Bring the stock to the boil, then turn the heat down and simmer for about 10 minutes. Add the tomatoes and simmer for another 10 minutes. Stir and check the consistency of the soup – add a splash more water if it seems too thick. Taste and adjust the seasoning, adding a squeeze of lemon juice if you think the soup needs it.

To make the gremolata, finely chop the lemon zest, garlic and coriander together until well combined.

Blend the soup if you want it smooth – the lentils will have broken down enough to thicken it, but there will still be some texture from the onions and tomatoes. Serve with the gremolata spooned over the top.

VEGGIE SCOTCH BROTH

A really hearty soup, this is a dish to enjoy on a night in by the fireside – and a guilt-free way to fill your sporran! There are plenty of vegetables, the peas and barley provide bulk and protein, while the mushroom ketchup adds a nice savouriness. The recipe makes a good big potful, but the soup keeps for several days and freezes well if you don't want to use it all at once.

100g pearl barley
100g split peas
1 large onion, diced
1 leek, trimmed and diced
3 celery sticks, diced
3 carrots, diced
½ small swede, diced
2 turnips, diced
½ small celeriac, diced
1 medium potato, diced
up to 1.5 litres vegetable stock
bouquet garni made up of 1 bay leaf, a sprig of parsley, a sprig of thyme
½ small savoy cabbage or similar quantity of kale, shredded
dash of mushroom ketchup
sea salt and black pepper

Rinse the barley and the split peas under cold running water, then put them in a large saucepan and add 750ml of water. Bring the water to the boil, boil fiercely for 15 minutes, then reduce the heat.

Add the onion, leek, celery and all the root vegetables, together with a litre of the vegetable stock and the bouquet garni. Season with salt and pepper and bring the soup back to the boil. Cover the pan and simmer for about an hour until the peas have started to break down and everything else is well softened.

Add the savoy cabbage or kale along with a dash of mushroom ketchup. Check the consistency – if you think the soup could do with more liquid, add more of the stock. Simmer for a few more minutes until the cabbage is nice and tender, then serve.

Serves 4 | 191 calories per serving | Prep: 10 minutes
Cooking time: up to 1 hour and 20 minutes (if using raw beetroots)

BEETROOT, FENNEL AND BLUE CHEESE SALAD

Beetroot and blue cheese are one of our favourite combos and we've put the blue cheese in the dressing here so you don't have to use a lot but you still get bags of flavour. We like to roast the beetroot, but if you're short of time it's fine to use vacuum-packed – you can use ready-cooked lentils too, if you like. Leave prepping the apples and pears to the last minute when you're assembling the salad so they don't go brown. Once you add the cheesy dressing they'll be fine.

4 medium beetroots
small bag of lamb's lettuce, well washed
100g puy lentils (or 200g ready cooked)
1 fennel bulb, cut into quarters and sliced
2 eating apples or pears
sea salt and black pepper

Blue cheese dressing
50g blue cheese, crumbled
150ml 0% fat yoghurt
¼ tsp runny honey
1 tsp cider vinegar
dash of Tabasco sauce

First roast the beetroots. Preheat the oven to 200°C/Fan 180°C/Gas 6. Put the beetroots in a roasting tray and cover them with foil. Cook them for an hour before testing for doneness – depending on size they will take anything between an hour and an hour and 20 minutes.

While the beetroots are roasting, cook the lentils – unless you're using ready-cooked ones. Put the lentils in a pan, cover them with water and bring to the boil. Turn down the heat and simmer the lentils until tender but still with a bit of bite to them, then drain and set them aside. They should take about 20 minutes, but check the packet instructions.

When the beetroots are tender, rub off their skins and cut them into wedges. Sprinkle with salt.

To make the dressing, mash the blue cheese until smooth, then gradually work in the yoghurt. Add the honey, cider vinegar and Tabasco, then season with salt and pepper. Add a few drops of warm water if the dressing seems too thick.

To assemble the salad, arrange the lamb's lettuce on 4 plates and add the lentils, fennel and beetroot. Peel and core the apples or pears and cut them into dice, then add them to the salad. Drizzle over the dressing and serve at once.

GADO GADO SALAD

There are lots of crunchy veggies in this fresh and flavoursome salad and they're all brought together with the peanut sauce – which is richly satisfying. Don't be tempted to leave out the shallot garnish, as it adds great taste and texture. This is fantastically healthy filler-upper of a dish.

100g baby new potatoes

100g green beans, trimmed and halved

½ Chinese cabbage, shredded

½ cucumber, cut into batons

1 large carrot, cut into thin batons

a few radishes, quartered lengthways

8 mushrooms, thickly sliced

2 tomatoes, cut into wedges

sea salt and black pepper

Peanut sauce

(see p. 36)

To garnish

1 tbsp vegetable oil

4 shallots, finely sliced

Bring a saucepan of water to the boil and add salt. Add the new potatoes and simmer them for 8 minutes, then add the green beans to the pan and cook for a further 3 minutes. When the potatoes are tender and the beans are still green and slightly al dente, drain them thoroughly and cool them all under running cold water. When the potatoes are cool enough to handle, slice them thickly.

Make the peanut sauce. Whisk all the ingredients together and season with salt and pepper. Set the sauce aside.

To make the garnish, heat the oil in a frying pan and add the shallots. Fry the shallots over a high heat, stirring very regularly, until they are a deep brown. Drain them on kitchen paper to get rid of any excess oil.

To assemble the salad, arrange the potatoes, beans and remaining vegetables over a large platter, keeping them separate from each other. Sprinkle with the fried shallots and drizzle over the peanut sauce before serving.

SMOKED TOFU, AVOCADO AND SPINACH SALAD

We used to make this with bacon, but now we've discovered smoked tofu we've realised the error of our ways. This salad is not only very tasty but also really nutritious. The quinoa and tofu provide protein and the avocado and spinach give you good fats and loads of vitamins. You can buy ready-cooked quinoa but it's so easy to cook yourself it's worth preparing a batch – you can freeze it too.

2 oranges

100g cooked quinoa (or about 35g raw weight)

200g baby spinach, washed

200g block of smoked tofu, diced

1 avocado, sliced

4 spring onions, shredded

Dressing

1 tsp wholegrain mustard

1 tbsp olive oil

juice from segmenting the oranges

juice of ½ lemon

sea salt and black pepper

First prepare the oranges. Take a thin slice off the top and bottom of each one, then stand them up on a flat surface and cut away the peel and outer layer of membrane from the sides, following the contour of the fruit. Holding a peeled orange over a bowl, cut it into segments, cutting down either side of the membranes, then squeeze the membranes out into the bowl. If there is quite a lot of flesh on the discarded skin, squeeze the juice from these too. Repeat with the other orange.

Arrange the quinoa over a large platter or in 4 individual bowls, then top with the spinach, tofu, avocado, spring onions and orange segments. To make the dressing, add the mustard, olive oil and lemon juice to the bowl with the orange juice and season. Whisk thoroughly, then drizzle over the salad.

To cook quinoa
Rinse the quinoa under cold running water – this helps remove any bitterness. Drain it well and tip it into a saucepan. Toast the quinoa over a medium heat without adding any liquid – this will help to dry it and also gives it a slightly nutty flavour. Cover with double the amount of water and add salt. Bring it to the boil, then cover the pan and simmer for 15–20 minutes. The quinoa should still have a very little bite to it. When cooked, quinoa should roughly triple in volume.

GOAT'S CHEESE, PEACH AND RADICCHIO SALAD

This salad is a reworking of one of our old favourites. Griddling radicchio really does make a big difference, reducing its bitterness and bringing a nice sweetness to the salad, so get your griddle out and enjoy. The rest is just an assembly job and the finished dish puts a smile on your face.

½ red onion, cut into very thin slices

4 heads of radicchio, trimmed

1 tbsp hazelnuts

handful of green salad leaves, such as watercress and rocket

2 peaches, cut into thin wedges

100g fresh goat's cheese, crumbled or broken into fairly small chunks

½ –1 red chilli, finely chopped

a few mint leaves

Dressing

1 tbsp olive oil

½ tsp mustard

¼ tsp honey

1 tsp cider vinegar

sea salt and black pepper

Put the slices of onion into a bowl of iced, salted water. Leave them until you are ready to assemble the salad, then drain them thoroughly. This gives them a milder flavour.

Preheat a griddle until it's too hot to hold your hand over. Cut each radicchio into quarters lengthways, making sure the leaves are still attached to the base. Set aside any leaves that do fall off. Grill the radicchio for 2–3 minutes on each side until they're slightly wilted and have deep char lines across them.

Toast the hazelnuts in a dry frying pan for a few moments, then roughly chop them.

Whisk all the dressing ingredients together with a tablespoon of water and season with salt and pepper. If the dressing is too thick, add a little more water.

To assemble the salad, spread the green leaves on a platter or divide them between 4 bowls. Top them with the drained red onion slices, peach wedges and the griddled radicchio.

Drizzle over the dressing and toss very lightly, without turning everything too much, then sprinkle over the goat's cheese, hazelnuts, chilli and mint leaves. Serve at once.

JUMBO COUSCOUS SALAD

Also known as giant couscous or Israeli couscous, jumbo couscous comes in larger pieces than the regular sort and has a more interesting texture. It's also toasted instead of dried so it has a nice nutty taste that we really enjoy. You could add a little chopped chilli to this salad if you're a fan or just a sprinkling of cayenne. Frozen peas and beans are fine here.

2 tsp olive oil
100g jumbo couscous
200g sprouting or tenderstem broccoli
100g peas
100g broad beans (or another 100g peas)
4 spring onions, sliced on the diagonal
100g watercress, roughly chopped
small bunch of mint, leaves only
a few tarragon leaves, finely chopped
sea salt and black pepper

Dressing
100ml low-fat yoghurt
pinch of saffron strands, soaked in 1 tbsp warm water
¼ tsp honey
pinch of caster sugar
a few finely chopped tarragon leaves

Put a teaspoon of the oil in a saucepan and add the couscous. Fry the cousous for a couple of minutes until it smells toasted, then cover it generously with salted water. Bring to the boil and simmer for 6–8 minutes, or until the couscous is just tender, then set it aside.

Bring a large saucepan of water to the boil, and add salt. Add the broccoli and blanch for 3 minutes, then remove it from the pan, run it under cold water and set aside. Add the peas and broad beans to the boiling water and cook for 2 minutes. Drain thoroughly and again, refresh under cold water.

Heat a griddle pan until it's very hot. Toss the broccoli in the remaining olive oil, then griddle it for a couple of minutes on each side until it's nicely charred. Cut the broccoli into short lengths when it's cool enough to handle.

Mix the couscous with the peas, broad beans and spring onions. Arrange the watercress over a large platter, then sprinkle the couscous mixture on top. Add the mint, tarragon and broccoli.

Whisk all the dressing ingredients together, including the saffron soaking water, then season with salt and pepper. Drizzle the dressing over the salad and serve immediately.

TOMATO, FETA AND WATERMELON SALAD

This is the most refreshing salad ever and a welcome treat on a hot day. There's only a small amount of dressing, as the ingredients are so juicy anyway, and the baked feta makes the whole thing into a tasty and satisfying dish.

Baked feta
200g feta cheese, cubed
1 tsp olive oil
juice and zest of ½ lemon
1 tsp smoked paprika
black pepper

Dressing
1 tbsp olive oil
1 tsp balsamic vinegar
sea salt and black pepper

Salad
100g bag of rocket or other salad leaves, washed
200g cherry tomatoes, halved
200g watermelon, cut into chunks and seeds removed
½ cucumber, cubed
a few black olives, pitted and sliced
small bunch of basil, leaves only

Preheat the oven to 200°C/Fan 180°C/Gas 6. Put the feta in a bowl, then add the olive oil, lemon juice and zest and the paprika. Season with pepper and toss gently so the feta is coated. Transfer the feta to an ovenproof dish and bake it for about 15 minutes until it is lightly golden brown on the outside and soft and creamy inside.

For the dressing, whisk the olive oil and balsamic vinegar together and season with salt and pepper.

Arrange the salad leaves on serving plates and drizzle with the dressing. Add the tomatoes, watermelon, cucumber and olives, then sprinkle over the basil leaves. Carefully place the baked feta cubes over the salad – they will break up if you handle them too roughly. Serve immediately.

GET PACKING –
LUNCH ON THE GO

NOODLE SALAD

SPAGHETTI WITH CHEESY COURGETTES AND GREENS

VEGETARIAN PASTIES

TOFU BLT

FALAFEL

PAN BAGNAT

SUCCOTASH

Serves 4 | 226 calories per serving
Prep: 20 minutes (plus pressing time) | Cooking time: 15 minutes

NOODLE SALAD

Nothing potty about this noodle salad and it's a great one to prepare at home to take to work for lunch. Full of flavour and goodness, it will keep you going and cheer up your lunch break. Look for firm or extra firm tofu, which will usually be in the chiller cabinet.

1 tsp vegetable oil
200g block of firm or extra firm tofu, pressed (see method)
100g mangetout
100g baby corn
100g asparagus
1 red pepper
½ cucumber
1 carrot
100g egg noodles
1 tsp sesame seeds
a few coriander leaves

Dressing
2 tbsp light soy sauce
1 garlic clove, finely chopped
15g fresh root ginger, grated
1 chilli, finely chopped
1 tsp rice vinegar
½ tsp honey
a few drops of sesame oil
sea salt and black pepper

Heat the oil in a frying pan. Cut the pressed tofu into cubes and fry them in the oil until golden-brown on all sides. Remove the cubes from the pan and leave them to cool.

Top and tail the mangetout and cut them into diagonal slices. Cut the corn into chunks and the asparagus into diagonal slices. Bring a pan of water to the boil and blanch them all for a minute, then drain and set aside.

Deseed and dice the pepper, cut the cucumber into small chunks and the carrot into thin sticks. Cook the noodles according to the packet instructions, then refresh them under cold running water.

To make the dressing, whisk all the ingredients together in a bowl and season with salt and pepper. Toss the noodles in the dressing, then add all the vegetables and the fried tofu. Sprinkle with the sesame seeds and coriander. Mix gently to combine, then divide the salad into 4 bowls or pack a portion into your lunch box. This salad will keep for a couple of days in the fridge.

Preparing tofu
To get the best results from tofu, drain it and press it before using. This firms up the texture by reducing the liquid content. Simply put the tofu between some sheets of kitchen paper. Cover it with a tray or plate and weigh it down with a couple of cans of tomatoes or beans. Leave the tofu for at least half an hour. Alternatively, put it in the fridge and leave it for several hours and it will continue to flatten and give out liquid.

SPAGHETTI WITH CHEESY COURGETTES AND GREENS

Th s is best eaten cold or at room temperature so makes an ideal packed lunch – a proper box of delights. And did you know that cold pasta is better for you than freshly cooked? Researchers have found that cold pasta doesn't raise your blood sugar as much as freshly cooked, so there you go!

150g wholemeal spaghetti

2 courgettes, spiralised or cut into long strips

100g peas

100g rocket or spinach, roughly chopped

75g low-fat cream cheese or ricotta

25g vegetarian Parmesan-style hard cheese, grated

zest of 1 lemon

1 garlic clove, crushed

small bunch of basil

sea salt

Bring a large pot of water to the boil and add salt. Cook the spaghetti until it's just al dente, adding the courgettes, peas and spinach or rocket for the last 30 seconds. Reserve a ladleful of the cooking liquid, then drain and tip everything back into the saucepan.

Add the cream cheese or ricotta, grated hard cheese, lemon zest and garlic and mix thoroughly. The sauce should just cling to the spaghetti without being thick or heavy – add a little of the reserved pasta water if you want to thin it out slightly.

When cooled, add the basil leaves and stir to combine. Serve in bowls or pack in your lunch box to take to work.

Makes 8 | 270 calories per pasty
Prep: 30 minutes (plus chilling time) | Cooking time: 50 minutes

VEGETARIAN PASTIES

Pies and pasties are what we're all about and we're never far from one – even when on a diet. Thankfully, our special potato pastry makes a pasty possible. These make a great dish for a picnic – or to take to work and enjoy watching the envy on your colleagues' faces. Bloomin' brilliant.

2 quantities of potato pastry (see p. 183)

1 egg, beaten, for sealing and glazing

Filling

100g celeriac, finely chopped

100g swede, finely chopped

1 small onion, finely chopped

50g reduced-fat Cheddar cheese, grated

1 tsp mushroom ketchup

½ tsp dried sage

sea salt and black pepper

Make the pastry and leave it to chill in the fridge for at least a couple of hours to firm up the dough. Preheat the oven to 200°C/Fan 180°C/Gas 6.

Bring a saucepan of water to the boil and add salt. Add the celeriac and swede and blanch for 2 minutes, then drain them and put them in a bowl. Leave them to cool completely, then add the onion, cheese, mushroom ketchup and sage. Season with salt and pepper and mix thoroughly.

Divide the dough into 8 pieces and roll each piece into a circle with a 12–13cm diameter – about the size of a saucer. Divide the filling into 8 portions. Take a circle of pastry and place a portion of filling in a line along the middle of the circle. Brush the exposed pastry with the beaten egg, then bring the 2 halves together, and seal, crimping the edges Cornish-pasty style. Repeat to make all the pasties, then brush them with beaten egg and place them on a baking tray lined with baking paper.

Bake the pasties in the oven for about 45 minutes until the pastry is golden brown and crisp. Transfer the pasties to a cooling rack to cool down so the underside of the pastry doesn't go soggy. Nice hot or cold.

Serves 4 | 286 calories per serving | Prep: 10 minutes (plus marinating time)
Cooking time: 15 minutes

TOFU BLT

Bacon, lettuce and tomato sandwiches are one of our favourite things, but we know we shouldn't be eating bacon too often. With this marinated smoked tofu you get almost the same lovely savoury smoky flavour but it's much better for you. Win, win, we say.

200g smoked tofu, cut into 12 thin slices
1 tbsp olive oil
8 thin slices of bread
low-fat mayonnaise, for spreading
leaves from a cos lettuce
2 large tomatoes, sliced
4 thin rounds of red onion (optional)

Marinade
1 tbsp chipotle paste
1 tbsp maple syrup
1 tbsp soy sauce
1 tsp mustard
sea salt and black pepper

Mix all the marinade ingredients together in a bowl and season with salt and pepper. Put the tofu slices on a plate and very carefully spread the marinade mixture over them, turning them over so they are completely coated. Leave them for at least half an hour, preferably longer, to marinate.

Heat the olive oil in a large frying pan and when it's hot, add the tofu slices and fry them for 2–3 minutes on each side until crisp round the edges.

Spread 4 of the slices of bread with a little mayonnaise. Layer on the tomatoes, onion, if using, add the tofu and lettuce and top with the remaining slices of bread.

Serves 4 | 406 calories per serving
Prep: 20 minutes (plus chilling time) | Cooking time: 25–30 minutes

FALAFEL

Everyone loves falafel, which are a bit of a trendy, hipster dish these days. Happily, our version won't stick to your hips! Falafel are easy to pack up and take to work to enjoy with some pitta and salad. You do need proper dried chickpeas, not canned, or you could use dried broad beans, which you can find in Middle Eastern food stores. A mixture of chickpeas and broad beans works well too.

200g dried chickpeas,
soaked overnight
2 tsp ground cumin
1 tsp ground coriander
½ tsp ground cinnamon
1 small red onion,
finely chopped
3 garlic cloves, chopped
small bunch of parsley,
small bunch of coriander,
juice of ½ lemon
1 tbsp plain flour
½ tsp baking powder
low-cal olive oil spray
sea salt and black pepper

Dressing
200ml low-fat yoghurt
1 tsp ground cumin
zest and juice of ½ lemon
½ tsp honey
1 tsp dried mint

To serve
4 small wholemeal pittas
slices of red onion,
cucumber and tomato
lettuce and coriander

Drain the soaked chickpeas thoroughly. Put two-thirds of them in a food processor and pulse until fairly smooth, pushing them down regularly with a spatula. Add the spices, onion, garlic, herbs, lemon juice, flour and baking powder, and the rest of the chickpeas. Season with plenty of salt and pepper, and continue to process until the mixture is well combined. You don't want it to be completely smooth – there should be plenty of texture. Chill the mixture for at least half an hour,

Preheat the oven to 180°C/Fan 160°C/Gas 4. Divide the mixture into 12 pieces. Roll these into balls and flatten them slightly or make them into the traditional torpedo shape if you prefer. Arrange the falafel on a baking tray and spray with low-cal oil. Bake them for 25–30 minutes until they're golden brown and beautifully crisp.

Meanwhile, make the dressing. Mix the yoghurt, cumin, lemon zest and juice, honey and dried mint together and season with plenty of salt and pepper.

Pile the falafel into pittas and add slices of red onion, cucumber and tomato and some lettuce and coriander leaves. Drizzle with some of the dressing, then enjoy.

Serves 4 | 300 calories per serving | Prep: 15 minutes (plus pressing time)
Cooking time: 10 minutes

PAN BAGNAT

You've got to try this one – the best, most flavoursome sandwiches from sunny Provence.
The name means 'bathed bread' and the rolls really do soak up all the lovely juices from the filling.
They actually improve if kept for a few hours after making so they're the ideal take-to-work or
picnic dish. Use your loaf – what's not to love?

4 ciabatta rolls
1 garlic clove, cut in half
2 roasted red peppers,
peeled and cut into strips
(peppers from a
jar are fine)
1 red onion, very
finely sliced
2 large tomatoes, sliced
½ cucumber, thinly sliced
25g green or black olives,
pitted and sliced
2 eggs, hard-boiled,
peeled and sliced
basil leaves

Dressing
1 tbsp olive oil
1 tsp red wine vinegar
1 tsp Dijon mustard
sea salt and black pepper

First, whisk together the dressing ingredients in a small bowl and season with salt and pepper. Set the dressing aside.

Cut the rolls in half, then scrape out most of the bread inside, just leaving the crust behind. You can use the discarded bread to make breadcrumbs for another dish. Rub the cut surface of the bread with the garlic clove.

Layer the remaining ingredients in the bottom half of the rolls. Start with some strips of red pepper, followed by slices of red onion, tomato, cucumber, olives and egg. Drizzle the dressing over the egg layer, then finish with some basil leaves.

Cover each roll with the top half, then press together. Wrap each roll tightly in baking paper, foil or cling film, then put them all in a bag and weigh them down – a couple of tins on top of a frying pan would work well here. Leave the rolls for about 10 minutes, then flip them over and press again. These can be eaten straight away, or can be kept for several hours before eating.

SUCCOTASH

This is our version of a dish that's long been popular in the US. It makes a great lunch box salad as it travels well and there's plenty of protein, thanks to the black-eyed beans.

200g broad beans

1 tsp vegetable oil

1 small onion, finely chopped

1 green pepper, deseeded and diced

200g sweetcorn (frozen is fine)

200g okra, trimmed and cut into rounds

2 garlic cloves, finely chopped

1 green chilli (preferably jalapeño, deseeded and finely chopped

400g can of black-eyed beans, drained

sea salt and black pepper

Tomato and basil dressing

2 medium tomatoes, finely chopped

1 tsp cider vinegar

pinch of sugar

small bunch of basil, shredded

½ tsp smoked paprika (optional)

Bring a pan of water to the boil and add the broad beans. Blanch them for 3 minutes, then drain, refresh under cold water and set them aside.

Heat the oil in a frying pan. Add the onion, green pepper, sweetcorn and okra, then season with salt and pepper. Cook over a medium heat for several minutes, stirring occasionally, until the vegetables are starting to soften and brown a little – the sweetcorn in particular should be browning.

Add the garlic and chilli, and cook for another couple of minutes, then remove the pan from the heat. Stir in the cooked broad beans and the black-eyed beans.

For the dressing, mix the tomatoes with the cider vinegar, sugar and the shredded basil. Pour this over the sweetcorn and bean mixture while it's still warm and sprinkle with smoked paprika, if using.

WE MISS MEAT – HEARTY DISHES

VEGETARIAN GARBURE

MUSHROOM, LEEK AND CHESTNUT PIE

MUSHROOM AND LENTIL RAGÙ

ROAST VEGETABLE LASAGNE

MEATLESS MEATBALLS

PROPER CHILLI

TOAD IN THE HOLE

VEGGIE BURGERS

VEGETARIAN LANCASHIRE HOTPOT

STUFFED CABBAGE ROLLS

MUSHROOM BOURGUIGNON

LATIN AMERICAN SHEPHERD'S PIE

Serves 8 | 337 calories per serving
Prep: 15 minutes (plus soaking time) | Cooking time: about 2 hours

VEGETARIAN GARBURE

Garbure is a thick cabbage soup that's popular in south-west France and usually contains ham. Our version is veggie but it still packs a punch. This recipe does make eight hearty portions but it keeps for a few days and freezes well so it's good to make a big batch. It's really worth using dried beans. All you have to do is remember to soak them the night before you want to make the dish.

500g dried cannellini beans, soaked overnight

1 onion, studded with 6 cloves

1 garlic bulb, broken into cloves, unpeeled

2 bay leaves

1 sprig of thyme

1 sprig of parsley

2 litres vegetable stock

1 tbsp mushroom ketchup

4 celery sticks, roughly chopped

4 turnips, cut into wedges

4 carrots, cut into thick chunks, diagonally

150g swede, cut into chunks

3 leeks, cut into chunks

1 small savoy cabbage, cut into wedges

sea salt and black pepper

Drain the soaked beans and put them in a large saucepan. Add the clove-studded onion, garlic, bay, thyme and parsley, then pour over 1½ litres of the stock and add the mushroom ketchup. Bring everything to the boil, then reduce the heat to medium and leave the soup to cook for 30 minutes.

Add the celery, turnips, carrots and swede, and season with salt and pepper. Bring the stock back to the boil, then turn down the heat to a lively simmer (somewhere between a boil and a simmer) and partially cover the pan. Cook for another hour until the beans and vegetables are close to tender.

Add the leeks and cabbage, pushing them down into the broth. If the garbure is looking very thick at this stage, add the rest of the vegetable stock. Partially cover the pan and cook for another 30 minutes, until the leeks and cabbage are tender when pricked with a fork, then remove the lid. Taste for seasoning and adjust if necessary. The garbure should be thick enough so you can almost stand your spoon up in it.

This is a main meal feast of a soup and low enough in calories that you can treat yourself to a bit of crusty bread alongside.

MUSHROOM, LEEK AND CHESTNUT PIE

There's nothing quite like a pie and this version is so tasty and comforting you won't even think about steak and kidney. We've made it top crust only to keep the calories down and we use our special potato pastry which we know you love. This makes a scrumptious family supper.

Filling
15g butter

2 leeks, sliced

350g chestnut or button mushrooms, sliced

2 garlic cloves, chopped

large sprig of thyme, leaves only

10g dried mushrooms, soaked in warm water for half an hour (optional)

1 tbsp plain flour

1 tsp Dijon mustard

100ml Marsala or red wine

200ml mushroom stock (see p. 180)

200g vacuum-packed chestnuts, left whole

Crust
1 quantity of potato pastry dough (see p. 183)

1 egg, lightly beaten

To make the filling, put the butter in a large saucepan and melt it over a low heat. Add the leeks, put a lid on the pan and leave the leeks to cook for 5 minutes. Turn up the heat slightly and add the mushrooms. Cook for another 4–5 minutes, then add the garlic and thyme. If using dried mushrooms, remove them from their soaking liquor, roughly chop them, then add them to the pan. Discard the soaking liquor.

Add the flour and stir until you see a roux has started to form around the vegetables. Stir in the mustard, then add the Marsala or red wine and stir until it is well incorporated. Gradually add the stock and bring the mixture to the boil, then turn down the heat and simmer, while stirring, until it has thickened. Add the chestnuts, cover, and remove the pan from the heat. Transfer the filling to a pie dish and leave it to cool. If you are using a deep pie dish, place a pie funnel in the centre.

Preheat the oven to 190°C/Fan 170°C/Gas 5. Roll the pastry out on a lightly floured work surface, until it is large enough to cover your pie dish. It will be fairly thin, about 3mm, but it will be robust enough that it won't break when you lift it.

Using your rolling pin, carefully lift the pastry and place it over the pie. Cut a hole for the pie funnel if you are using one. Wet the rim of the pie plate with water and press the pastry firmly on to it, then trim the edges and crimp them. For a good colour, glaze the pie with beaten egg. Bake the pie in the preheated oven for 40–45 minutes until the crust is a deep golden brown. Serve with some green veg.

Serves 6–8 | 302 calories per serving (6); 226 calories per serving (8)
Prep: 15 minutes | Cooking time: about 1 hour

MUSHROOM AND LENTIL RAGÙ

This is a great alternative to the usual meaty Bolognese sauce to serve with your pasta – it's good for lasagne too. We like to include lentils, but you can also use quorn or a combo of the two. If you want to use just quorn, add 500g.

250g puy or brown lentils
1 tbsp olive oil
1 onion, finely chopped
2 celery sticks, finely chopped
1 large carrot, finely chopped
250g mushrooms, finely chopped
2 garlic cloves, finely chopped
1 tsp dried oregano
200ml red wine
1 tbsp tomato purée
400g can of chopped tomatoes
sea salt and black pepper

To serve
50g linguine or spaghetti per person
shavings of vegetarian Parmesan-style hard cheese (optional)

Cook the lentils according to the packet instructions, then set them aside. Be careful not to overcook them – they should still have a little bite so they don't collapse when added to the sauce.

Heat the olive oil in a saucepan. Add the onion, celery and carrot and a splash of water. Cover the pan with a lid and fry the vegetables gently, stirring regularly, for at least 10 minutes until they have softened. Add the mushrooms and garlic, turn up the heat slightly and cook until any liquid coming from the mushrooms has evaporated. Sprinkle in the oregano followed by the cooked puy lentils.

Pour in the red wine and cook fiercely until most of it has evaporated, then add the tomato purée and the canned tomatoes. Season with salt and pepper. Bring to the boil, then turn down the heat, cover the pan and simmer for about 20 minutes. Remove the lid and if the sauce seems too liquid, cook uncovered for another 5 minutes.

Serve with linguine or spaghetti – a 50g serving will add about 180 calories to your total – and a little Parmesan-style cheese if you like.

Serves 6 | 241 calories per serving (with leeks); 343 calories per serving (with dried lasagne)
Prep: about 30 minutes | Cooking time: 1 hour and 15 minutes

ROAST VEGETABLE LASAGNE

We knew this was a keeper when Andrew, our photographer, pinched the leftovers to take home for supper. You can replace the pasta with leek leaves if you want to lower the calorie count and either way it tastes fantastic – a real treat for the family. Even the pasta version isn't too high cal.

1 aubergine, halved lengthways and cut into crescents

200g piece of pumpkin or squash, sliced into thin wedges

1 large red onion, cut into thin wedges

2 red peppers and 1 green pepper, deseeded and cut in half

1 garlic bulb, cloves separated

1 tsp dried oregano

low-cal oil spray

sea salt and black pepper

To assemble

2 large leeks, trimmed or 150g dried lasagne

1 quantity of tomato sauce (see p. 178)

1 quantity of béchamel sauce (see p. 177)

50g low-calorie Cheddar cheese, grated

25g vegetarian Parmesan-style hard cheese, grated

Preheat the oven to 200°C/Fan 180°C/Gas 6. Arrange the aubergine, pumpkin or squash, onion, peppers and garlic over 2 roasting tins or trays. Sprinkle with the oregano and spray with oil. Roast the veg for 25–30 minutes until they are charred in places and just cooked through, then remove them from the oven. Squeeze the flesh from the garlic cloves and chop it roughly. When the peppers are cool enough to handle, skin them and cut the flesh into strips.

If using pasta, cook it according to the packet instructions. If using leeks, trim them to the same width as your lasagne dish. Cut them through the middle, then take the larger leaves from the outside of the leeks. Bring a large pot of water to the boil and add salt. Add the leek leaves and simmer them for 5 minutes or until very tender. Drain the leaves and cool them under cold running water, then lay them out on kitchen paper or a clean tea towel to absorb any excess liquid.

To assemble the lasagne, spoon half the tomato sauce over your lasagne dish and top with half the roasted vegetables. Spoon over a very little of the béchamel sauce and top with leek leaves or pasta sheets, making sure everything is covered. Repeat this until you have used up all the tomato sauce, vegetables and leek or pasta sheets. Cover with the remaining béchamel, then sprinkle with the grated cheese.

Bake in the oven for 40–45 minutes until the cheese is a rich golden brown and the lasagne is piping hot.

MEATLESS MEATBALLS

There's nothing like a meatball and these veggie versions have just the same lovely comforting mouthfeel as the meaty kind. This makes a fab supper dish that all the family will love.

100g brown lentils
1 tbsp olive oil
1 small onion, finely chopped
1 medium carrot, grated
100g spinach or chard, washed and finely shredded
1 garlic clove, finely chopped
1 tsp cumin
½ tsp cinnamon
½ tsp cardamom
50g breadcrumbs
25g pine nuts, lightly crushed
zest and juice of 1 lemon
2 tbsp finely chopped parsley
1 egg, beaten
sea salt and black pepper

Sauce

1 quantity of tomato sauce (see p. 178)
1 tbsp harissa paste
small bunch of parsley, finely chopped
squeeze of lemon juice

First cook the brown lentils according to the packet instructions and set them aside in a bowl. If using ready-cooked lentils, you need 250g.

Preheat the oven to 200°C/Fan 180°C/Gas 6. Heat the olive oil in a frying pan and add the onion and carrot. Cook them over a low heat until the onion has softened, then add the spinach or chard. Continue to cook until the greens have wilted and softened – if using spinach, cook it until any liquid evaporates. Add the garlic and cook for another minute, then add the spices. Season with salt and pepper.

Add the breadcrumbs, pine nuts, lemon zest and juice and the parsley to the bowl with the lentils, then the cooked vegetables. Stir in the egg and the mixture should clump together. Form the mixture into 12 balls of about 40g each and arrange them on a baking tray. Bake them in the oven for 10–12 minutes until lightly browned.

Put the tomato sauce in a large, shallow flameproof casserole dish or a deep frying pan and stir in the harissa paste, some of the parsley and a squeeze of lemon juice. Add the lentil and spinach balls in a single layer. Cover the dish with a lid and heat through on the hob for a few minutes until everything is piping hot. Sprinkle with the rest of the parsley and serve at once.

PROPER CHILLI

A good chilli is one of our Friday night favourites and we've discovered you can make an excellent version with quorn instead of beef mince. It tastes the business and it's much lower in calories, which means you can treat yourself to some garnishes, such as cheese and crème fraiche.

1 tsp vegetable oil
1 red onion, chopped
1 large red pepper and
1 green pepper,
deseeded and diced
2 celery sticks, diced
4 garlic cloves, finely
chopped
500g quorn mince
1 tsp oregano
1 bay leaf
1 tbsp ground cumin
1 tbsp chipotle paste
200ml red wine
400g can of chopped
tomatoes
250ml vegetable stock
400g can of kidney
beans, drained
15g dark chocolate
sea salt and black pepper

To serve
lime wedges
fresh coriander, chopped
half-fat crème fraiche
(optional)
75g reduced-fat Cheddar
cheese, grated

Heat the oil in a large, flameproof casserole dish or in a saucepan, then add the onion, peppers and celery. Cook them over a low heat for 5 minutes, until they're starting to soften, then add the garlic and the quorn mince. Turn up the heat and quickly brown the quorn. Add the oregano, bay leaf, cumin and chipotle paste and stir until the vegetables and quorn are well coated with the spices and paste.

Pour in the red wine and allow it to bubble up and boil off, then add the tomatoes and vegetable stock. Add the drained beans and season with salt and pepper.

Bring everything to the boil, then cover the pan and leave the chilli to simmer over a low heat for 20 minutes. Remove the lid and continue to simmer gently for another 10 minutes to reduce and thicken the sauce. Add the chocolate for the last 5 minutes, stirring until it has melted into the sauce.

Serve the chilli with rice or cauliflower rice and as many of the garnishes as you like.

TOAD IN THE HOLE

We really are chuffed with this one and it's a great example of how veggie recipes can be lower in calories than the meaty originals. If you don't want to make your own sausages, use one of the supermarket versions. And for a real feast, serve with our onion gravy (see page 179).

Vegetarian sausages

10g butter

1 onion, finely chopped

200g mushrooms, very finely chopped

3 garlic cloves, finely chopped

½ tsp dried sage

½ tsp dried thyme

300g potatoes, very finely diced

1 tsp mushroom ketchup

1 tsp tomato ketchup

2 tbsp plain flour

1 egg, beaten

50g breadcrumbs

low-cal oil spray

sea salt and black pepper

Yorkshire pudding

100g plain flour

2 eggs

200ml semi-skimmed milk

10ml vegetable oil

To serve

onion gravy (see p. 179)

First make the sausages. Melt the butter in a frying pan. Add the onion and mushrooms and fry until the mushrooms have given out their liquid, then keep going until the pan is dry. Add the garlic, sage and thyme and cook for a few more minutes.

While the onions and mushrooms are frying, bring a saucepan of water to the boil and add the potatoes and some salt. Simmer for 3–4 minutes, watching carefully – you want the potatoes to hold their shape and not be at all mushy. Drain them well.

Lightly crush the potatoes – they should have some texture, not be mashed to a purée. Fold them into the mushroom mixture together with the mushroom and tomato ketchups. Season to taste, then put the mixture in the fridge for a while to firm up.

Preheat the oven to 200°C/Fan 180°C/Gas 6. Shape the mixture into 8 sausages. Put the flour, beaten egg and breadcrumbs in separate bowls. Dip each sausage in the flour, dust off any excess, then dip it into the egg and roll it in the breadcrumbs. Spray a roasting tin with oil and add the coated sausages. Spray them again with oil and bake them in the oven for 20 minutes.

To make the Yorkshire pudding, whisk the flour, eggs and milk in a bowl and season with salt. Leave the batter to stand while the sausages are cooking. Take the sausages out of the oven and add the oil to the tin. Put the tin back in the oven for the oil to heat up, then remove it and quickly pour in the batter around the sausages. Pop the tin back in the oven and cook for another half an hour until the batter is well risen and golden brown.

Serves 8 | 412 calories per serving
Prep: 20 minutes (plus chilling time) | Cooking time: 30 minutes

VEGGIE BURGERS

We've experimented with loads of different recipes for veggie burgers and this is our favourite. Plenty of flavour, great texture and the beetroot gives the whole thing a pleasingly meaty look. Try our special burger buns made with potato dough too. They're brilliant, though we say it ourselves.

1 tsp vegetable oil
1 red onion, finely chopped
2 garlic cloves, finely chopped
2 x 400g cans of black beans, roughly mashed
100g cooked brown rice
2 small cooked beetroots, coarsely grated
1 tbsp tomato purée
1 tsp mushroom ketchup
1 tsp soy sauce
1 tsp onion powder
50g fine breadcrumbs
sea salt and black pepper

To cook and serve
low-cal oil spray
8 slices of reduced-fat hard cheese (optional)
8 burger buns (see p. 182)
lettuce leaves
2 tomatoes, sliced
1 red onion, sliced
gherkins, sliced

Heat the oil in a frying pan, add the onion and cook until it's very soft and lightly caramelised. Add the garlic and cook for another couple of minutes, then take the pan off the heat, tip the onion and garlic into a bowl and leave them to cool.

Add the remaining burger ingredients to the cooled onion and garlic. Season well with salt and pepper, then put the mixture in the fridge to chill for a couple of hours. Shape the mixture into 8 patties weighing about 100g each, then put them in the fridge again until you are ready to cook. You can also freeze the burgers at this stage: open freeze them until firm, then transfer them to a freezer-proof container.

When you are ready to cook the burgers, preheat the oven to 200°C/Fan 180°C/Gas 6. Spray a baking tray with low-cal oil. Arrange the burgers on the baking tray, spray them with a little low-cal oil, then bake them for 20 minutes. If using cheese, add it for the last 3–4 minutes of the cooking time.

Lightly toast the burger buns, then layer up the burgers with the salad ingredients and any condiments you like.

You could also add smoked tofu to your burgers instead of cheese. It's best to marinate and grill the tofu as for the TLT (see page 86).

Serves 4 | 333 calories per serving | Prep: 25 minutes | Cooking time: about 1 hour and 45 minutes

VEGETARIAN LANCASHIRE HOTPOT

We've done classic hotpots, we came up with a brilliant sausage version and this is our latest – a Lancashire hotpot with vegetarian black pudding. And it's good – Dave's a Lancashire lad and he wouldn't put up with anything but the best. Our mams would be proud.

1 tsp vegetable oil
2 onions, finely sliced
1 tbsp flour
750ml vegetable stock
1 tsp dried sage
1 tsp mushroom ketchup
500g potatoes, thinly sliced
250g swede, thinly sliced
1 apple, finely diced
250g vegetarian black pudding, peeled and sliced
10g butter
sea salt and black pepper

Heat the oil in a large frying pan and add the onions with a splash of water. Cook them for a few minutes until they're starting to soften, then sprinkle over the flour and stir until the onions are completely coated with the flour. Add the stock, together with the sage and the mushroom ketchup, and simmer until the liquid has reduced and thickened slightly.

Preheat the oven to 180°C/Fan 160°C/Gas 4. Divide the potatoes into 3 piles. Arrange a layer of potatoes and half the swede and apple in the base of a casserole dish. Add half the black pudding, then season with salt and black pepper. Pour over half the onion sauce. Add the second pile of potato and the remaining swede, apple, black pudding and onion sauce. Top with the final batch of potatoes, then dot with the butter.

Put the lid on the casserole dish and cook the hotpot in the preheated oven for an hour. Remove the lid and cook for another 30 minutes or until the top layer of potatoes is crisp and golden. Serve with some green vegetables and you'll have a real treat.

Serves 4–6 | 378 calories per serving (4); 252 calories per serving (6)
Prep: 30 minutes | Cooking time: about 1 hour and 30 minutes

STUFFED CABBAGE ROLLS

We're really happy with this one. Vegetarian haggis is a great product that works brilliantly as a stuffing for the cabbage, and the mushroomy sauce is the perfect partner. A very satisfying supper.

1 large savoy cabbage
1 vegetarian haggis

Sauce
1 tsp olive oil
5g butter
2 shallots or 1 small onion, finely chopped
400g mushrooms, finely chopped
2 garlic cloves, finely chopped
1 sprig of thyme
1 tsp dried oregano
100ml vermouth or white wine
200g chopped tomatoes
100ml vegetable stock
sea salt and black pepper

First make the sauce. Heat the olive oil and butter in a saucepan and add the shallots or onion. Cook over a gentle heat until they're starting to soften, then add the mushrooms. Turn up the heat and cook for a few minutes, then add the garlic and cook for another 2 minutes.

Add the herbs, then pour over the vermouth or white wine. Bring to the boil and allow most of the liquid to evaporate, then add the tomatoes and stock. Season with salt and pepper, then bring everything back to the boil. Turn down the heat and simmer for about 20 minutes until you have a rich sauce.

To make the rolls, take 12 leaves from the cabbage and trim them, cutting out any thick, woody stems from the base. Bring a large saucepan of water to the boil, add the cabbage leaves and blanch them for 2–3 minutes until they're soft and pliable, but still fresh and green. Remove the leaves and allow them to cool, then dry them well. Preheat the oven to 200°C/Fan 180°C/Gas 6.

Remove the haggis from its wrapping and cut it into 12 even slices. Shape each slice into a cylinder. Take a cabbage leaf and place a piece of the haggis across it, close to the bottom of the leaf. Fold in the sides of the leaf, then roll it up, enclosing the slice of haggis. Repeat with the remaining leaves and haggis.

Cover the base of a shallow ovenproof dish with a third of the sauce. Arrange the stuffed cabbage rolls over the sauce – they should fit fairly snugly. Pour the rest of the sauce around them. Cover the dish with foil and bake in the oven for about an hour, then serve piping hot.

Serves 4–6 | 200 calories per serving (4); 133 calories per serving (6)
Prep: 25 minutes | Cooking time: 50–60 minutes

MUSHROOM BOURGUIGNON

This is so rich and delicious you don't miss the meat at all. We like to use a selection of mushrooms as listed, but you can just use one sort if that's what you have. Serve this with pasta if you like, but it's also great alongside a potato and celeriac dauphinoise (see page 174) or simply spooned over a baked potato — not one the size of a football though. Don't forget you're watching the calories.

15ml olive oil

12 button onions or shallots, peeled

500g portobellini mushrooms, thickly sliced

250g chestnut mushrooms, halved

250g large white button mushrooms, halved

15g butter

1 onion, very finely chopped

1 carrot, very finely chopped

1 celery stick, very finely chopped

2 sprigs of thyme

1 sprig of rosemary

1 bay leaf

3 garlic cloves, finely chopped

1 tbsp plain flour

250ml red wine

250ml mushroom stock (see p. 180)

1 tbsp tomato purée

sea salt and black pepper

Heat the olive oil in a large frying pan and add the button onions or shallots. Fry them over a high heat until they're browned on all sides, then put them on a plate. Add all the mushrooms to the pan and cook them very briskly until they are lightly browned but are not releasing any liquid. Remove the pan from the heat and set it aside.

Heat the butter in a large saucepan or a flameproof casserole dish. Add the finely chopped onion, carrot and celery, together with the thyme, rosemary and bay leaf. Cover the pan and cook for 15 minutes until the vegetables have softened, then remove the lid and continue to cook until everything is lightly caramelised. Add the garlic and cook for a further minute, then season well with salt and pepper.

Sprinkle the flour over the vegetables and stir, then pour in all the wine. Stir to combine, making sure nothing catches on the bottom, then leave to simmer until the wine has reduced by half. Add the stock and tomato purée and stir until the tomato purée has dissolved into the sauce. Add the cooked mushrooms and onions or shallots, then bring the mixture back to the boil.

Turn the heat down and simmer for about 15 minutes, until the onions or shallots are tender and the sauce has reduced down. Serve with pasta or a dauphinoise (see page 174) and some green vegetables.

Serves 4–6 | 400 calories per serving (4); 266 calories per serving (6)
Prep: 25 minutes | Cooking time: about 1 hour and 15 minutes

LATIN AMERICAN SHEPHERD'S PIE

This is a winner – a good old shepherd's pie turns Latin, with a sweetcorn topping instead of mash. Make this and it won't just be the pie that's full of beans. The filling is a delight of spicy loveliness, but you could also try using the chilli recipe on page 106 if you fancy a change. There isn't a lot of topping – we're keeping the calories down – so use a fairly deep dish.

1 large red onion
2 celery sticks
1 large carrot
1 red pepper and 1 green pepper, deseeded
1 tsp vegetable oil
2 garlic cloves, chopped
1 tbsp ground cumin
1 tsp ground coriander
½ tsp cinnamon
½ tsp smoked chilli powder (chipotle)
2 tbsp finely chopped coriander stems
400g can of kidney beans
400g can of butter beans
400g can of tomatoes
300ml vegetable stock
sea salt and black pepper

Topping
500g sweetcorn kernels
3 tbsp fine cornmeal (polenta) or plain flour
1 tsp baking powder
15g butter
50g reduced-fat Cheddar cheese, grated

To make the filling, finely chop the onion and celery and dice the carrot and peppers. Heat the vegetable oil in a large saucepan and add all the vegetables, along with a splash of water. Cover the pan and leave the veg to cook gently until soft – this should take about 15 minutes. Add the garlic, spices and coriander stems and stir to combine.

Add all the beans, then pour over the tomatoes and the stock. Season with salt and pepper, then bring everything to the boil. Reduce the heat and leave to simmer until the sauce is well reduced, then tip everything into a deep oven dish. Preheat the oven to 190°C/Fan 170°C/Gas 5.

To make the topping, blitz half of the sweetcorn kernels in a food processor with the cornmeal or flour, baking powder and butter until smooth. Season with plenty of salt, then add the remaining sweetcorn and blitz again to make a mixture with a rough, dropping consistency.

Spread the topping evenly over the filling and sprinkle with the grated cheese. Bake the pie in the oven for 30–40 minutes until the topping is a deep golden-brown and the filling is piping hot.

THE MAIN EVENT

VEGETABLE LAKSA

PANEER AND PEA CURRY

RED KIDNEY BEAN AND GREEN BEAN CURRY

SWEET POTATO SAAG ALOO

VEGGIE TACOS

TOFU STIR-FRY

COURGETTE CAPONATA PASTA

CAULIFLOWER AND BROCCOLI CHEESE

BARLEY RISOTTO WITH GREENS

GARLICKY BEAN AND TOMATO STEW

ROAST VEGETABLE TRAY BAKE

CAULIFLOWER PILAF WITH LENTILS AND BROAD BEANS

STUFFED AUBERGINES

CHRISTMASSY COBBLER

SPICED VEGETABLE STRUDEL

BUDDHA BOWLS

VEGETABLE LAKSA

Once you've got all the ingredients together it's very easy to make the laksa paste for this dish (see page 178), but if you don't fancy the idea you can buy a small jar of ready-made. Check it's suitable for vegetarians though – many contain shrimp paste, fish sauce and chicken stock. If you're not a strict vegetarian you could add a dash of fish sauce to your laksa for extra flavour.

1 tsp vegetable oil

250g button mushrooms (or a selection of exotic mushrooms), halved if large

laksa paste (see p. 178) or use a small jar of ready-made paste

400ml can of reduced-fat coconut milk

600ml vegetable stock

2 Kaffir lime leaves, finely shredded

1 carrot, peeled and cut into matchsticks

100g baby corn

up to 1 tbsp soy sauce

100g rice vermicelli

200g Chinese greens

100g beansprouts

juice of 1 lime

sea salt and black pepper

To serve

small bunch of mint and small bunch of coriander, roughly chopped

Heat the oil in a large flameproof casserole dish or a wok. When the oil is shimmering, add the mushrooms and stir-fry them for a minute or so just to seal and brown them lightly, then turn down the heat and add the laksa paste. Stir for another minute or so, then pour in the coconut milk and stock.

Add the lime leaves, carrot and baby corn, then simmer for 5 minutes. Season with salt and pepper and add a dash of soy sauce to taste. Cook the rice vermicelli according to the packet instructions.

Add the greens to the broth and cook for another couple of minutes, then add the beansprouts and cooked vermicelli. Simmer for a moment, then add the lime juice. Taste for seasoning and add salt and pepper as necessary.

Serve the laksa in bowls and sprinkle with plenty of mint and fresh coriander.

PANEER AND PEA CURRY

Paneer is a kind of set cottage cheese that features in many Indian vegetarian dishes and you can buy it in supermarkets now. Here it's used in a great curry, with lots of warm spicy flavours. We do love our curries and this one's definitely a winner. It has a nice low calorie count so you could serve it with some rice, a chapati or one of the other curries in this chapter.

1 tbsp vegetable oil or ghee

2 onions, sliced

30g fresh root ginger, grated

3 garlic cloves, crushed

1 tbsp Kashmiri chilli powder

2 tsp ground cumin

1 tsp ground coriander

½ tsp ground fenugreek

½ tsp ground turmeric

½–1 tsp cayenne pepper

400g can of tomatoes or passata

juice of ½ lemon

250g paneer, cubed

150ml low-fat yoghurt

100g peas

freshly chopped coriander, to garnish

sea salt and black pepper

Heat a teaspoon of the oil or ghee in a deep frying pan and add the onions with a splash of water. Sauté the onions over a medium heat until they're softened and starting to brown, then add the ginger and garlic. Cook for another couple of minutes, then add the spices and stir to coat the onion. Add the tomatoes and lemon juice, season with salt and pepper, then leave to simmer for 10 minutes.

Transfer the sauce to a blender or food processor and blitz until smooth. Set the sauce aside.

Heat the remaining oil in the frying pan. Add the paneer and fry it on all sides until lightly browned. Pour over the sauce, then add the yoghurt and peas. Stir to combine and add a splash more water if the sauce seems too thick. Simmer for a few more minutes, then garnish with coriander before serving.

RED KIDNEY BEAN AND GREEN BEAN CURRY

As you know, we like a bit of spice and we've used whole spices in this curry for the best colour and texture and a good fiery flavour. If you're worried by whole spices and bits of cinnamon stick in your food you could use a teaspoon of curry powder instead.

1 tsp coriander seeds

seeds from 1 tsp cardamom pods

15ml coconut oil, vegetable oil or ghee

a few curry leaves (optional)

3cm piece cinnamon stick

2 cloves

1 large onion, finely sliced

3 garlic cloves, finely chopped

30g fresh root ginger, finely chopped

1 tsp ground cumin

1 tsp cayenne

¼ tsp ground turmeric

½ tsp ground fenugreek

1 tomato, finely chopped

400ml reduced-fat coconut milk

2 x 400g cans of red kidney beans, drained

200g green beans, trimmed

fresh coriander leaves, roughly chopped

sea salt and black pepper

Roughly crush the coriander seeds and cardamom seeds. Heat the oil in a large flameproof casserole dish. Add the curry leaves, if using, the crushed coriander and cardamom seeds and the cinnamon and cloves. Fry until the spices start to sputter, then add the onion. Continue to fry quite briskly until the onion is golden brown, then add the garlic, ginger and ground spices.

Cook for another couple of minutes, then add the chopped tomato. Season with salt and pepper and cook until the tomato starts to break down. Pour in the coconut milk, then add the kidney beans. Simmer for 10 minutes, adding a little water if the sauce is reducing too much – you want it to stay fairly thin – then add the green beans Simmer for another 5 minutes.

Serve the curry garnished with plenty of chopped coriander.

SWEET POTATO SAAG ALOO

Saag aloo is usually made with regular potatoes but we like our sweet potato version. The great thing about these little beauties is they are richer in nutrients – particularly vitamin C – than white potatoes and lower in starch. They count towards your five a day too, while regular potatoes don't. We like to make our own spice mix for this but if you prefer you can use curry powder.

1 tbsp vegetable oil

1 onion, thinly sliced

2 garlic cloves, finely chopped

20g fresh root ginger, grated

1 tbsp spice mix (see below) or mild curry powder

2 sweet potatoes, diced

1 tomato, diced

300ml vegetable stock

150–200g bag of baby spinach, picked over and thoroughly washed

squeeze of lemon juice

sea salt and black pepper

Spice mix

1 tsp coriander seeds

1 tsp cumin seeds

1 tsp fennel seeds

½ tsp ground turmeric

To serve

a few green chillies, sliced

a few sprigs of coriander

If making the spice mix, toast the whole spices lightly in a frying pan, then grind them to a powder. Mix with the turmeric.

Heat the oil in a large flameproof casserole dish or a deep frying pan. Add the onion and cook it quite briskly until it's softened and very lightly browned. Add the garlic, ginger and the spice mix or curry powder and stir until combined.

Add the sweet potatoes to the pan and stir to coat them with the garlic, ginger and spices, then add the tomato and the vegetable stock. Season with salt and pepper. Bring the stock to the boil, then turn down the heat, cover the pan and simmer very gently until the sweet potato is just cooked. This should take no longer than 10 minutes, but check regularly from 5 minutes as you don't want the sweet potato to go mushy – it should still have a little bite to it. Loosen the sauce with a little more stock or water if necesssary.

Add the spinach to the pan and cover the pan again until the spinach has wilted down. Stir very carefully to combine without breaking up the sweet potatoes. Add a squeeze of lemon juice and serve garnished with green chillies and fresh coriander.

VEGGIE TACOS

These tacos are a veggie delight. We like to do the whole number with refried beans and lots of toppings and they make a brilliant fiesta of flavour to share with friends.

Refried beans

1 tsp vegetable oil

1 red onion, finely chopped

2 garlic cloves, finely chopped

1 tsp dried oregano

2 x 400g cans of black or pinto beans, drained

250ml vegetable stock or water

sea salt and black pepper

Veggie filling

1 tsp vegetable oil

100g sweetcorn

1 red pepper, deseeded and cut into strips

1 red onion, cut into thin wedges

200g butternut squash or pumpkin, diced

1 tbsp tomato purée

1 tsp chipotle paste (or more, depending on how hot you like it)

100g kale, cavolo nero or chard, shredded

First make the refried beans. Heat the vegetable oil in a medium saucepan or a deep frying pan. Add the onion with a splash of water, cover the pan and sauté until the onion has softened and turned golden brown.

Add the garlic and oregano and cook for another couple of minutes. Add the beans and plenty of salt and pepper. Pour the stock or water into the pan, then mash the beans with a potato masher or the back of a wooden spoon until about half of them are broken up. Simmer over a gentle heat, stirring to prevent the mixture catching on the bottom, until you have a thick purée. Keep warm or reheat gently just before you serve the tacos.

For the filling, heat the oil in a large, lidded frying pan. Add the sweetcorn, red pepper, red onion and squash or pumpkin, then cook over a high heat, stirring infrequently so the vegetables build up a bit of colour on each side. The texture should be still al dente, with a light charring or browning around the edges.

Stir in the tomato purée and chipotle paste and season with salt and pepper. Add 200ml of water, then pile the greens on top. Cover and simmer for several minutes until the greens are cooked through, then stir everything together.

For the crema, mash the avocado with the lime juice and a generous pinch of salt. Put the avocado in a small food processor with the coriander and crème fraiche or soured cream and blitz until the mixture is smooth but still flecked.

Avocado crema

1 avocado

juice of 1 lime

a few coriander leaves

2 tbsp half-fat crème fraiche or soured cream

To serve

8 corn tortillas

½ red onion, finely chopped

a few coriander leaves

lime wedges

To serve, heat the tortillas in a dry frying pan or a pancake pan until they're very lightly browned on each side. Keep them warm – a basket lined with a tea towel to fold over the tortillas works very well.

To eat, spread some of the refried beans over the base of a tortilla, then top with some veggie filling, avocado crema, red onion, a few coriander leaves and a squeeze of lime.

TOFU STIR-FRY

Everyone loves a stir-fry and once you've got all the chopping out of the way this is so quick and easy to make. The tofu gives you plenty of protein – and frying it makes it tasty. If you want extra carbs you could serve this with steamed rice or noodles.

up to 2 tbsp vegetable oil

2 x 200g blocks of tofu, pressed (see p. 81) and cut into cubes

1 tsp cornflour

200g shiitake mushrooms, sliced

1 red pepper, deseeded and sliced into strips

200g asparagus, trimmed and cut into short lengths

4 spring onions, sliced diagonally

2 garlic cloves, finely chopped

2 red chillies, finely sliced

10g fresh root ginger, finely chopped

200g Asian greens (pak choi or tatsoi)

2 tbsp light soy sauce

1 tbsp mirin

½ tsp honey

a few drops of sesame oil

1 tsp sesame seeds

Heat a tablespoon of the vegetable oil in a wok. Put the tofu cubes in a bowl and toss them with the cornflour. When the air above the oil is shimmering, add the tofu and stir-fry until it is golden brown and crisp on all sides – this shouldn't take longer than a couple of minutes. Remove the tofu from the wok with a slotted spoon and set it aside.

Add a little more oil to the wok if needed. Add the mushrooms, red pepper and asparagus to the pan and stir-fry for 2 minutes, then add the spring onions, garlic, chilli and ginger. Continue to cook for another 2 minutes, then add the greens.

Pour over the soy sauce, mirin and honey, then put the tofu back in the wok. Leave to cook until the greens have wilted down, then serve immediately, garnished with a few drops of sesame oil and the seeds.

Serves 4 | 133 calories per serving (sauce only); 314 calories per serving (with pasta);
Prep: 20 minutes | Cooking time: 35–40 minutes

COURGETTE CAPONATA PASTA

Caponata is a punchy vegetable dish that can be eaten on its own but it's also great with pasta. Do remember to weigh your pasta – it's easy to get carried away, as we know all too well. The veg for caponata are sometimes left quite chunky, but for serving with pasta we like to chop everything a bit more finely. If you like, you can add 50g of chopped green olives along with the capers and these will add an extra 20 calories per person.

1 tbsp olive oil
2 red onions, diced
2 red peppers, diced
3 large courgettes, diced
2 garlic cloves, finely chopped
1 tsp chilli flakes
grated zest of 1 lemon
¼ tsp cinnamon
400g can of chopped tomatoes
1 tbsp red wine vinegar
1 tsp honey
2 tbsp capers, rinsed
sea salt and black pepper

To serve
200g pasta, such as penne or shells
small bunch of parsley, finely chopped

Heat the olive oil in a large saucepan and add the onions and peppers. Stir to coat them in the oil, then put a lid on the pan and cook over a low heat for about 10 minutes until the vegetables are softened.

Turn up the heat and add the courgettes. Fry briskly for about 5 minutes, until everything starts to brown a little but the courgettes are still firm. Add the garlic, chilli flakes, lemon zest and cinnamon, then stir briefly.

Pour the tomatoes into the pan with a splash of water and add the vinegar, honey and capers. Season with salt and pepper, bring the mixture to the boil again, then turn the heat down and cover the pan. Leave the sauce to simmer for 10 minutes, then remove the lid and cook uncovered for another 5 minutes.

Cook the pasta according to the packet instructions and serve with the sauce and plenty of chopped parsley.

CAULIFLOWER AND BROCCOLI CHEESE

Cauli cheese is a big warm cuddle of a dish. We've adapted this favourite by adding extra flavours to the sauce and reducing the amount of cheese to make it less calorific. And the mix of broccoli and cauliflower makes the dish look really special. Some roasted tomatoes go well with this.

600ml semi-skimmed milk

1 slice of onion

2 cloves

1 bay leaf

1 cauliflower (500–600g, trimmed weight), broken into florets

1 head of broccoli (about 300g), broken into florets

20g cornflour

1 heaped tsp wholegrain mustard

50g reduced-fat Cheddar cheese, grated

2 tbsp finely chopped parsley

sea salt and black pepper

Topping

25g reduced-fat Cheddar, cheese, finely grated

1 tbsp fine breadcrumbs

Pour the milk into a saucepan and add the onion, cloves and bay leaf. Heat until the milk is just coming up to the boil, then remove the pan from the heat and leave the milk to infuse while you cook the vegetables.

Bring a large saucepan of water to the boil. Add a good pinch of salt and the cauliflower and cook for 3 minutes. Add the broccoli to the pan and cook for another 2 minutes. Check for doneness. The cauliflower and broccoli should be tender but still have a little bite to them – al dente, as they say. Drain the vegetables thoroughly and put them in a large ovenproof dish. Preheat the oven to 200°C/Fan 180°C/Gas 6.

Strain the milk into a jug, then rinse out the saucepan and pour the milk back in. Mix the cornflour with a little cold water in a small bowl and stir until you have a smooth, thin paste. Put the pan of milk back over the heat and pour in the cornflour mixture. Gradually bring the sauce to the boil, stirring constantly until it has thickened. Add the mustard, cheese and parsley to the sauce and stir until the cheese has melted, then pour it over the cauliflower and broccoli.

Mix the cheese and breadcrumbs together to make the topping and sprinkle it over the sauce. Bake in the oven for 20–25 minutes until well browned and bubbling. Fantastic!

BARLEY RISOTTO WITH GREENS

Barley is not just for Scotch broth. It makes a great risotto and is a nice change from risotto rice. It's packed full of minerals and vitamins too, so let's eat more of it. You can also make this tasty dish with spelt if you fancy.

1 tsp olive oil
10g butter
1 onion, finely chopped
2 garlic cloves, finely chopped
1 tsp fresh thyme leaves
zest of 1 lemon
200g pearl barley, rinsed
100ml white wine
1 litre vegetable stock
400g tenderstem or sprouting broccoli, trimmed and cut into chunks
100g runner beans, shredded, or broad beans
100g peas
sea salt and black pepper

To finish
25g vegetarian Parmesan-style hard cheese, grated (optional)
handful of basil, shredded

Heat the olive oil and butter in a saucepan, then add the onion and cook it over a gentle heat for a few minutes until it's starting to soften. Add the garlic and cook for another minute, then add the thyme, lemon zest and barley. Stir until the grains look glossy, then pour over the wine. Bring it to the boil and let most of the wine boil off, then pour in the stock. Season with salt and black pepper.

Bring the stock to the boil, then turn the heat down and simmer gently, stirring regularly to make sure the barley doesn't catch on the bottom of the pan.

Meanwhile, bring a large saucepan of water to the boil and add salt. Add the broccoli and beans and simmer for 2 minutes. Add the peas and cook for another minute, then drain everything into a colander.

When most of the liquid has been absorbed by the barley, check the texture – if the grains aren't quite done, add a little more liquid if necessary. When you are happy the barley is cooked, beat in the cheese, if using, then fold in all the greens. Garnish with basil and serve.

GARLICKY BEAN AND TOMATO STEW

A knockout dish, this makes a hearty supper. There's a double whammy of garlic here – creamy cooked garlic in the stew and raw garlic in the garnish, so you'll be in no danger from vampires.

10ml olive oil
1 onion, thinly sliced
1 carrot, sliced
2 celery sticks, thickly sliced
100ml white wine
1 litre vegetable stock
1 garlic bulb
rind of vegetarian Parmesan-style hard cheese (optional)
1 tsp dried oregano
1 sprig of rosemary
2 leeks, sliced into rounds
150g butternut squash, diced
400g can of cannellini beans or chickpeas
25g short pasta
3 tomatoes, chopped
bunch of cavolo nero, shredded
100g green beans, topped
sea salt and black pepper

Herb garnish
bunch of basil and bunch of parsley, chopped
2 garlic cloves, chopped
1 tbsp olive oil

Heat the olive oil in a large saucepan or a flameproof casserole dish and add the onion, carrot and celery. Add a splash of water, cover the pan and cook for about 10 minutes until the vegetables have softened and are starting to colour. Add the white wine and stock, then the garlic – break it into cloves but leave them unpeeled. Add the cheese rind, if using, the oregano and rosemary and season with salt and pepper.

Bring everything to the boil, cover the pan and simmer for 5 minutes, then add the leeks, squash, beans or chickpeas and pasta. Simmer for a further 5 minutes then add the tomatoes, cavolo nero and green beans. Continue to simmer, covered, until the pasta is al dente and the vegetables are just tender.

To make the garnish, put the herbs, chopped garlic cloves and oil in a small food processor and process until well combined. If the mixture seems too thick and hard to work, add a splash of the vegetable cooking liquid to the processor. Season the garnish with salt and pepper.

To serve, fish out the cheese rind, if you added one. You can also remove the garlic cloves, squish them out of their skins and put them back in the stew, or you can let everyone do this for themselves at the table. Serve the stew with the herb sauce to drizzle over.

ROAST VEGETABLE TRAY BAKE

Everyone loves a tray bake and here's a great one for you. Roasting vegetables always adds loads of flavour and while the oven works its magic you can put your feet up. Then all you have to do is whizz up the dressing and tuck in.

½ small cauliflower

1 large aubergine, cut into chunks

1 red and 1 green pepper, deseeded and cut into thick strips

2 onions (red or white), cut into thin wedges

200g piece of squash or pumpkin, thickly sliced

2 small courgettes, sliced

1 garlic bulb, broken into cloves

1 tbsp olive oil

zest of 1 lemon

400g can of chickpeas, drained

sea salt and black pepper

Green tahini dressing

1 tbsp olive oil

1 tbsp tahini

1 tbsp pomegranate molasses

small bunch of coriander or parsley

Preheat the oven to 200°C/Fan 180°C/Gas 6.

Break the cauliflower into fairly small florets and put them with the rest of the vegetables in a large roasting tin. Season them with plenty of salt and pepper, then drizzle over the olive oil and sprinkle with lemon zest. Add 100ml of water to the tin, then pop the veg into the preheated oven and roast them for 40 minutes until they have softened and are starting to char a little around the edges.

Take the tin out of the oven and give everything a good stir, then add the chickpeas. Put the tin back in the oven for another 10 minutes.

To make the dressing, put all the ingredients in a small food processor. Remove the garlic cloves from the roasting tin and squeeze the creamy flesh into the food processor, discarding the skins. Blitz until you have a fairly smooth but green-flecked purée and season with salt and pepper. Loosen the dressing with a little water if it seems too thick.

Serve the vegetables and chickpeas with the tahini dressing to drizzle over.

CAULIFLOWER PILAF WITH LENTILS AND BROAD BEANS

You can get great caulis all year round in Britain now. We don't think we eat enough of this excellent vegetable so here's another one of our experiments with cauli 'rice'. This pilaf is packed with spicy flavour and makes a tasty supper. Serve it on its own or with one of the vegetarian curries – probably best to leave out the lentils if you do this.

10g butter or 10ml vegetable oil

1 large onion, thinly sliced

2 garlic cloves, crushed

5g fresh root ginger, finely chopped

5 cardamom pods

2 x 3cm pieces of cinnamon stick

1 tsp cumin seeds

1 tsp fennel seeds (optional)

3 cloves

2 bay leaves

1 medium cauliflower (about 750g)

generous pinch of saffron, soaked in 100ml warm water

150g baby broad beans

100g cooked brown lentils (optional)

Heat the butter or oil in a large, lidded frying pan or a shallow flameproof casserole dish. Add the onion with a splash of water, cover the pan and cook the onion, stirring every so often, until it has softened. Add the garlic and ginger, fry for another couple of minutes, then add the whole spices and the bay leaves.

While the onions are softening, prepare the cauliflower. Break it into florets, then blitz them in a food processor until the cauli resembles coarse breadcrumbs. Add these to the pan with the onions, then pour over the saffron and its soaking liquid.

Cook for about 5 minutes, stirring regularly, until the liquid has evaporated and the cauliflower is fluffy.

Bring a small pan of water to the boil and blanch the broad beans for 3 minutes. Drain them and run them under cold water to cool them, then pop the beans out of their skins. Add these to the cauliflower along with the lentils, if using.

To make the dressing, mix all the ingredients together and season with salt and pepper.

For the garnish, chop the herbs and toast the almonds lightly in a dry frying pan. Fold the herbs through the pilaf and sprinkle with the almonds and pomegranate seeds. Drizzle with the dressing and serve warm.

Dressing

100ml low-fat yoghurt

1 tbsp tahini

1 tbsp pomegranate
molasses

1 garlic clove, crushed

squeeze of lemon juice

sea salt and black pepper

To serve

small bunch of parsley

small bunch of dill

small bunch of mint

25g flaked almonds

seeds from ½
pomegranate

STUFFED AUBERGINES

There are lots of big bold flavours in the stuffing for these aubergines, plus an awesome grain called freekeh. Freekeh is young wheat that has been roasted and cracked and it has a good nutty taste. It's also high in fibre, protein and nutrients so well worth a try – you'll find it in most supermarkets.

2 large aubergines
low-cal olive oil spray
50g freekeh
1 tbsp olive oil
1 red onion, finely chopped
2 garlic cloves, finely chopped
2 tsp ras el hanout or 1 tbsp harissa paste
generous pinch of saffron, soaked in a little water
zest and juice of 1 lemon
1 tomato, finely chopped
½ tbsp pomegranate molasses
small bunch of parsley, finely chopped
a handful of mint leaves, finely chopped
½ tsp preserved lemon, finely chopped
2 tbsp breadcrumbs
sea salt and black pepper

Preheat the oven to 200°C/Fan 180°C/Gas 6. Slice the aubergines in half lengthways, then cut out most of the flesh, making sure you leave a border of about ½ cm. Finely chop the flesh and set it aside. Spray the shells with oil and season them with salt and pepper, then put them in a roasting tin and cover with foil. Roast the aubergines in the oven for 20 minutes.

Soak the freekeh in cold water for 5 minutes. Drain it thoroughly, rinse again under running cold water, then put it in a saucepan. Cover it with water, add salt, then bring to the boil. Turn the heat down, cover the pan, then simmer the freekeh gently for about 15 minutes. Remove the pan from the heat and leave the freekeh to stand for 5 minutes, then drain. The freekeh should be al dente – still with a little bite to it.

Heat the olive oil in a frying pan and add the onion and the aubergine flesh. Sauté them over a gentle heat for several minutes until soft, then add the garlic. Cook for another couple of minutes, then add the ras el hanout or harissa paste and the saffron, lemon zest and juice, tomato and pomegranate molasses. Add 100ml of water and season. Simmer for a few minutes until the tomato has collapsed down and the aubergine is cooked, then add the freekeh and all but 2 tablespoons of the parsley and the mint. Spoon the stuffing into the aubergines.

Mix the rest of the herbs, preserved lemon and breadcrumbs together with a crack of black pepper and sprinkle this over the stuffed aubergines. Bake the aubergines in the oven for 25–30 minutes until the filling is hot and the tops are well browned.

Serves 6 | 577 calories per serving | Prep: 30 minutes
Cooking time: 1 hour and 30 minutes

CHRISTMASSY COBBLER

This does have a festive feel but it's a nice warming dish to serve on any winter night. We've taken some classic Christmas ingredients, such as sprouts and chestnuts, and turned them into a properly indulgent feast. To complete the Christmassy vibe, serve with cranberry sauce (see page 177).

3 large parsnips
200g celeriac
3 carrots
12 button onions, peeled and left whole
250g Brussels sprouts, trimmed and halved
100ml vermouth or white wine
1 tsp dried thyme
low-cal oil spray
300ml single cream
300ml whole milk
1 bay leaf
1 slice of onion
2 cloves
grating of nutmeg
1 heaped tsp plain flour
sea salt and black pepper

Cobbler topping
200g self-raising flour
2 tsp baking powder
50g cold butter, cubed
100g chestnuts, crumbled
1 egg
125ml buttermilk

Preheat the oven to 200°C/Fan 180°C/Gas 6. Cut the parsnips and celeriac into bite-sized chunks and the carrots into thin diagonal slices. Put all the vegetables in a large roasting tin and season them with salt and pepper. Pour over the vermouth or wine and sprinkle with the thyme. Cover the dish with foil and roast the vegetables in the oven for 35–40 minutes until they are just tender when pierced with a knife. Remove the foil and spritz the vegetables with oil, then roast for a further 10–15 minutes to brown slightly. Transfer the roast vegetables to a deep ovenproof dish and leave the oven on.

Meanwhile, put the cream and milk in a saucepan along with the bay leaf, onion, cloves and nutmeg. Bring almost to the boil, then remove the pan from the heat and leave the cream and milk to infuse.

Strain the cream and milk infusion, then whisk in the flour. Pour this over the vegetables and stir briefly.

To make the topping, put the flour and baking powder in a bowl and add salt. Rub in the butter with your fingertips, then stir in the chestnuts. Beat the egg and buttermilk together, then mix briefly with the dry ingredients to make a sticky dough.

Drop tablespoons of the cobbler mixture over the top of the vegetables, spacing them out as much as possible. Bake in the oven for about 30 minutes, until the topping is well risen and brown. Serve with cranberry sauce (see page 177).

SPICED VEGETABLE STRUDEL

Some veggies and a good hit of spice all wrapped up in filo pastry – this is a real treat. It looks impressive but it's not difficult to make and we know you're going to love it.

1 tsp vegetable or coconut oil

1 large onion, finely chopped

1 tsp mustard seeds

1 tsp nigella seeds

2 turnips, finely diced

2 carrots, finely diced

200g cauliflower, broken into small florets

2 garlic cloves, finely chopped

10g fresh root ginger, finely chopped

1 tbsp curry powder

100g chickpeas, from a can, lightly crushed

small bunch of coriander, finely chopped

25g reduced-calorie hard cheese, grated

5 large sheets of filo pastry

low-cal oil spray

Heat the oil in a large frying pan. Add the onion, mustard seeds and nigella seeds and fry for several minutes until the onion has softened. Bring a saucepan of water to the boil and add the turnips and carrots. Simmer them for 3 minutes, then add the cauliflower florets. Cook for a further minute, then drain all the veg thoroughly and set them aside.

Add the garlic, ginger and curry powder to the onions in the frying pan and cook for a couple of minutes. Add the blanched vegetables, along with the chickpeas and coriander. Pour over 250ml of water and simmer until most of the water has evaporated. Add the grated cheese and stir until it has melted. Remove the pan from the heat and leave the mixture to cool.

Preheat the oven to 200°C/Fan 180°C/Gas 6.

Lay a sheet of filo on a large baking tray. Spray it with low-cal oil, then place another sheet of filo on top. Continue until you have a pile of 5 sheets, spraying with oil in between each one. Spoon the cooled mixture down the length of the filo, just to one side of the middle. Wet the borders and turn in the short sides. Turn in the smallest of the long borders, then roll the filo up, leaving it seam-side down.

Spray with the low-cal oil again to help the filo brown in the oven. Bake the strudel in the oven for about 30 minutes until it's crisp and a light golden brown. Nice with a green salad and some lime pickle or mango and yoghurt dressing (see page 58).

BUDDHA BOWLS

This is our version of bibimbap, a favourite dish in Korea and one that we first ate when we travelled there. It might look a bit complicated but it's not – all you're doing is cooking the various bits and pieces separately and popping them in a low oven to keep warm. Then you assemble your banging big bowl of goodies. Up to you if you want to add kimchi – Korean fermented vegetables – or not. It's so popular here now you can buy it in supermarkets.

150g brown rice
200g block of firm tofu, pressed (see p. 81)
low-cal oil spray
1 tsp vegetable oil
250g shiitake mushrooms (or a selection), quartered
100g asparagus tips
2 garlic cloves, thinly sliced
1 tbsp mirin
3 large carrots
2 slices of fresh root ginger (no need to peel)
250g pak choi
100g beansprouts
sea salt

To serve
4 eggs
soy sauce
sesame oil
1 tsp black sesame seeds
a few sprigs of coriander leaves, torn
2 spring onions, finely chopped
chilli sauce (optional)
kimchi (optional)

Preheat the oven to 120°C/Fan 100°C/Gas ½. Rinse the rice and put it in a saucepan with plenty of cold water. Bring the water to the boil, and cook the rice until tender – this will probably take about 20 minutes, but check the packet instructions.

While the rice is cooking, cut the tofu into thick strips. Spray a frying pan with low-cal oil and fry the strips of tofu for a few minutes on each side until golden brown. Spray an oven dish with oil and add the tofu. Cover the dish with foil and put it in the oven.

Heat the teaspoon of oil in a frying pan or a wok and add the mushrooms and asparagus. Cook them briskly over a high heat, stirring regularly, until the mushrooms are glossy and brown and the asparagus is still al dente. Add the garlic and some salt and cook for another couple of minutes, then add the mirin and toss everything together.

Remove the dish of tofu from the oven and add the mushrooms and asparagus, keeping them separate from the tofu, then cover the dish again and put it back in the oven.

Cut the carrots into batons. Bring a saucepan of water to the boil and add salt and the ginger. Simmer the carrots for several minutes until they're just tender, then remove them from the saucepan with a slotted spoon and add them to the oven dish with the mushrooms. Bring the cooking water back to the boil.

Trim the pak choi and cut them into quarters lengthways. Add them to the pan of water and simmer until the leaves have wilted, then drain.

Spray the frying pan with low-cal oil, add the eggs and fry them until the whites are just set.

While the eggs are frying, assemble the bowls. Divide the rice between 4 bowls. Dress it with a little soy sauce and a few drops of sesame oil. Remove the dish from the oven and arrange a quarter of the carrots, the mushroom and asparagus mixture, tofu, pak choi and beansprouts in each bowl, keeping each element separate. Dress with more soy sauce. Add a fried egg to each bowl, then drizzle with sesame oil and sprinkle over a few sesame seeds, coriander leaves and spring onions.

Serve with more soy sauce, chilli sauce and kimchi if you like.

PUDDINGS AND BAKES

INSTANT BANANA ICE CREAM

PEAR AND GINGER GALETTE

STEAMED PUDDING

CHOCOLATE BEETROOT CAKE

STRAWBERRY AND ORANGE SALAD

AZTEC CHOCOLATE AVOCADO MOUSSE

PUMPKIN, RUM AND RAISIN ICE CREAM

SPICED APPLE MUFFINS

Serves 4–6 | 129 calories per serving (4); 86 calories per serving (6)
Prep: 10 minutes (plus freezing time)

INSTANT BANANA ICE CREAM

This sounds bonkers but it's brilliant. It's the speediest ice cream ever and tastes like a real treat, even though it contains very little fat and sugar. All you need to do is think ahead and get the bananas into the freezer and then you can whip up a pud in no time.

4 very ripe bananas

juice of ½ lime

grated zest of ½ lime, plus extra to garnish

½ tsp cinnamon, plus extra to garnish (optional)

a few drops of vanilla extract

2 tbsp soft light brown sugar or maple syrup

100ml yoghurt or half-fat crème fraiche

Peel the bananas and cut them into fairly small chunks. Toss the chunks in the lime juice and arrange them on a baking tray. Put them in the freezer and leave them until they're completely solid all the way through – this will take at least 2 hours, but leave them overnight if possible.

Put the frozen bananas in a food processor with the lime zest, cinnamon, vanilla extract, sugar or maple syrup and the yoghurt or crème fraiche. Blend until the mixture is thick, smooth and creamy, then serve sprinkled with some extra lime zest and cinnamon if you like.

PEAR AND GINGER GALETTE

Pears and ginger are great together and perfect for this fruity little beauty. It might look quite rough and ready but that's fine and it tastes heavenly. You'll need a jar of those little balls of stem ginger in syrup – you only need one for this but they keep for ages and you can use them in the avocado mousse on page 166 too. We like to use spelt flour in the pastry for this, as it adds a lovely nutty flavour that goes well with the pears.

1 quantity of potato pastry (see p. 183), made with spelt instead of white flour, well chilled

flour, for dusting

juice of ½ lemon

3 or 4 firm pears (not too ripe)

1 tbsp soft muscovado sugar

1 piece of stem ginger, rinsed and finely chopped

1 tsp ground ginger

pinch of ground cinnamon

pinch of ground cardamom

grating of nutmeg

10g butter

1 egg, beaten, to glaze

To serve

half-fat crème fraiche

Preheat the oven to 200°C/Fan 180°C/Gas 6. Roll out the pastry into a large circle – it doesn't matter if it's a bit rough around the edges, as it's fine for the finished dish to look a little rustic. Lightly dust a baking tray with flour, then carefully transfer the rolled out pastry on to it.

Put the lemon juice in a bowl. Peel and core the pears, then slice them into thin wedges. Add the wedges to the bowl of lemon juice as you go, turning them regularly. This will stop the pears going brown. Mix the sugar, stem ginger and spices together in a bowl. Sprinkle this mixture over the pear slices and mix everything thoroughly but gently – you don't want the pear slices to break up.

Arrange the pears in the centre of the pastry, making sure you leave a 5cm border around the edge. Pour over any sugary liquid left in the bowl. Dot with the butter, then fold the border of pastry over the pears, leaving most of them exposed. Brush the pastry with the beaten egg.

Bake the galette in the preheated oven for 35–40 minutes until the pastry is crisp and golden brown. Serve warm with spoonfuls of crème fraiche.

Serves 6 | 238 calories per serving (without custard)
Prep: 15 minutes | Cooking time: about 2 hours

STEAMED PUDDING

The inspiration for this was a pudding that was popular during the Second World War when ingredients such as sugar, butter and eggs were rationed. The pudding included grated veg so we've incorporated that idea in a slightly richer recipe. It's a bit like Christmas pud but far lower in calories – still high in tastiness though.

50g currants
50ml Marsala (or apple juice)
100g plain flour
50g breadcrumbs
25g vegetable suet
1 tsp baking powder
1 tbsp mixed spice
75g soft dark brown sugar
150g carrots, finely grated
1 small eating apple, cored and grated
1 egg
pinch of salt
cake-release spray or butter, for greasing

Put the currants in a small saucepan and cover them with the Marsala or apple juice. Bring to the boil, then remove the pan from the heat and leave the currants to infuse.

Mix all the other ingredients (except the cake-release spray or butter) together in a bowl. Add the currants with any remaining liquid and combine.

Spray a 750ml pudding basin with cake-release spray or grease it very lightly with butter. Scrape the mixture into the basin, then cover with pleated foil and tie the foil in place with string or fasten with a rubber band.

Stand the pudding in a steamer over a large saucepan – or if you don't have a steamer, fold up a small tea towel, put it in the saucepan and place the pudding on top of that. Add boiling water to about halfway up the sides of the pudding basin and put a lid on the pan. Steam the pudding in simmering water for about 2 hours, checking the water level regularly and making sure the pan doesn't boil dry. Always top up with boiling water.

When the pudding is cooked, turn off the heat and lift the basin from the water. Leave it to stand for 5 minutes. Remove the foil, run a palette knife around the edge of the basin to loosen the pudding, then turn it out on to a plate. Serve with custard if you like.

Makes 12 slices | 188 calories per slice
Prep: 15 minutes | Cooking time: 50–60 minutes

CHOCOLATE BEETROOT CAKE

Beetroot works amazingly well in a cake and helps to give a lovely rich, brownie-like texture – yum! This is sheer indulgence, but cut the cake into small slices and you'll keep the calorie count reasonable. Vacuum-packed beets work fine here and save you a bit of time.

75ml groundnut or vegetable oil, plus extra for greasing
200g cooked beetroot
200ml full-fat yoghurt
175g self-raising flour
1 tbsp baking powder
50g cocoa
100g golden caster sugar
1 tsp vanilla extract (optional)
50g dark chocolate chips OR 50g dark chocolate, chopped or coarsely grated

To serve
crème fraiche (optional)
extra cocoa powder, to sprinkle (optional)

Preheat the oven to 180°C/Fan 160°C/Gas 4. Grease a deep 20cm cake tin with a little oil and line it with baking paper.

Put the beetroot in a food processor and blitz it until smooth. Add all the remaining ingredients, except the chocolate chips or chocolate, then pulse until you have a smooth batter, scraping the mixture down a couple of times if necessary.

Fold the chocolate chips or chopped chocolate into the batter, then spoon the batter into the cake tin.

Bake the cake in the preheated oven for 50 minutes to 1 hour, until it's well risen, springy to the touch and has shrunk slightly away from the sides. Don't rely on the clean skewer test for this one, as the beetroot keeps the cake moist and you might encounter a molten chocolate chip.

Remove the cake from the oven and leave it to cool in its tin for about 10 minutes, then turn it out on to a cooling rack. Sprinkle it with a little cocoa powder if you like. Serve slightly warm – the chocolate will remain melted – or cold with crème fraiche.

STRAWBERRY AND ORANGE SALAD

You don't always have to serve strawberries with high-cal cream. We like our berries with some nicely segmented oranges and seasoned with a touch of balsamic vinegar and black pepper – quick, fragrant and tasty. Trust us and give this one a go.

300g strawberries, hulled and halved
1 tsp caster sugar
2 oranges
1 tsp balsamic vinegar
grinding of black pepper
a few mint leaves

Put the strawberries in a bowl. Sprinkle the sugar over them and set aside for a few minutes to let the sugar dissolve.

Take a thin slice off the top and bottom of one of the oranges, then stand it up on a flat surface and cut away the peel and outer layer of membrane from the sides, following the contour of the fruit. Take the peeled orange in your hand and hold it over the bowl containing the strawberries to catch any juice. Cut out the orange segments, cutting as close as you can to the membrane. Put the segments in a bowl (not in with the strawberries yet). Repeat the process with the other orange.

Take the orange peel trimmings and the discarded membranes and squeeze them over the strawberries to get every last bit of juice. Sprinkle over the vinegar and a little black pepper, then leave the salad to stand for an hour at room temperature.

To serve, combine the macerated strawberries with the orange segments and garnish with a few mint leaves.

AZTEC CHOCOLATE AVOCADO MOUSSE

Dave first came across this treat in California. It's simple and quick to make but success depends on using very ripe, creamy, non-fibrous avocados. Good Hass avocados are probably best. You need a jar of stem ginger in syrup and you could use some of the syrup in the mousse instead of honey.

2 avocados, peeled and roughly mashed

zest and juice of ½ lime

1 ball of stem ginger, roughly chopped

100g dark chocolate (70% cocoa solids)

50g honey (or syrup from the stem ginger)

100ml reduced-fat coconut milk

30g cocoa

1 tsp ground cinnamon

1 tsp ground ginger

¼ tsp ground allspice

¼ tsp ground cayenne

To serve

1 ball of stem ginger, finely sliced (optional)

Put the avocado, lime zest and juice and the piece of stem ginger in a food processor and blitz until fairly smooth – there might be a little texture from the stem ginger or lime zest.

Put the chocolate, honey or syrup, coconut milk, cocoa and spices in a small saucepan. Place the pan over a very gentle heat and whisk constantly until the chocolate has melted and you have a rich, dark mixture.

Scrape the chocolate mixture into the food processor with the avocado, lime and ginger and continue to blitz until everything is well combined and smooth. Divide the mousse between 6 or 8 small glasses, espresso cups or bowls and chill until needed.

Serve topped with some thin strips of stem ginger if you like.

PUMPKIN, RUM AND RAISIN ICE CREAM

Who knew veggie dieting could be this much fun? Pumpkin makes epic ice cream and goes beautifully with the spices, rum and raisins in this recipe. We find this works best when frozen in a loaf tin, then cut into slices – like the old-fashioned Neapolitan ice cream we used to love as kids! Use tinned unsweetened pumpkin purée, which you can buy in supermarkets.

75g raisins
75ml rum
400ml whole milk
1 tsp ground cinnamon
1 tsp ground ginger
½ tsp ground allspice
¼ tsp ground nutmeg
pinch of cloves
60g soft light brown sugar
25g maple syrup
200ml double cream
175g unsweetened pumpkin purée (from a can)

Put the raisins in a small saucepan and cover them with the rum. Bring to the boil, then remove the pan from the heat and leave the raisins to infuse. They should plump up and absorb most of the rum.

Put the milk in another saucepan. Mix the spices with the sugar, then add this to the milk together with the maple syrup. Heat slowly until the sugar has dissolved into the milk, then bring to the boil. Remove the pan from the heat, pour the mixture into a bowl and leave it to cool down completely.

Whisk the cream in a bowl until it's thick and forming soft peaks, then whisk this into the milk and sugar mixture along with the pumpkin purée. Add the raisins and any remaining rum and stir well.

Line a loaf tin with cling film and scrape in the ice cream. Put the tin in the freezer and leave until the ice cream is solid. Remove the ice cream from the freezer 20–30 minutes before you want to serve it and transfer it to the fridge. Cut the ice cream into slices to serve.

Makes 12 muffins or 24 fairy cakes | 220 calories per muffin; 110 calories per fairy cake

Prep: 15 minutes | Cooking time: 20–25 minutes

SPICED APPLE MUFFINS

Even when you're dieting there are times when only a bit of cake will do and these spicy muffins go down a treat with a cup of tea. They are reasonably low in calories but if you like, you could make 24 little fairy cakes instead of 12 muffins. Just watch you don't eat double the number!

cake-release spray (optional)

300g plain flour

2 tsp baking powder

½ tsp bicarbonate of soda

2 tsp ground cinnamon

½ tsp ground nutmeg

pinch of cloves

200ml whole milk

60g full-fat yoghurt

60ml vegetable oil

100g light soft brown sugar

2 eggs

2 large eating apples, finely diced

50g porridge oats

Preheat the oven to 200°C/Fan 180°C/Gas 6. Line a muffin tray or fairy cake tins with paper cases or spray the tins with cake-release spray.

Put the flour into a bowl with the baking powder, bicarbonate of soda and spices, then whisk thoroughly to combine.

Put the milk, yoghurt, oil, sugar and eggs in a separate, larger bowl and whisk to combine. Add the flour mixture and most of the apples and oats to the wet ingredients, stirring briefly to combine. Try to keep stirring to a minimum as over-working the batter can give a tough result.

Divide the mixture between the cases – you will find the mixture will come almost to the top of them. Sprinkle over the remaining apple and oats.

Bake in the preheated oven for 20–25 minutes until well risen, golden brown and firm to the touch. Remove the cakes from the oven and place them on a rack to cool.

SIDE DISHES AND BASICS

POTATO AND CELERIAC DAUPHINOISE

QUICK CUCUMBER SALAD

ROOT VEGETABLE ROSTI

RAINBOW VEGETABLE 'COUSCOUS'

BÉCHAMEL SAUCE

CRANBERRY SAUCE

TOMATO SAUCE

LAKSA PASTE

ONION GRAVY

BASIC VEGETABLE STOCK

MUSHROOM STOCK

SPRING VEGETABLE STOCK

POTATO BREAD BURGER BUNS

POTATO PASTRY

Serves 6–8 | 206 calories per serving (6); 154 calories per serving (8)
Prep: 15 minutes | Cooking time: up to 1 hour and 20 minutes

POTATO AND CELERIAC DAUPHINOISE

300ml whole milk

2 garlic cloves, 1 thinly sliced, 1 cut in half

1 sprig of thyme

500g potatoes, very thinly sliced

500g celeriac (1 medium), thinly sliced

200ml half-fat crème fraiche

2 tsp plain flour

15g butter

sea salt and black pepper

Put the milk in a small saucepan with the sliced garlic and the thyme. Bring the milk almost to the boil, then remove the pan from the heat and leave the milk to infuse until cool.

Preheat the oven to 160°C/Fan 140°C/Gas 3. Rub the cut garlic over the base of a large ovenproof dish. Layer the potatoes and celeriac in the dish, seasoning with salt and pepper between each layer. Strain the milk into a jug and whisk in the crème fraiche and the flour.

Pour the liquid over the potatoes and celeriac, then dot with butter. Cover the dish with foil and bake for half an hour in the preheated oven. Remove the foil and bake the dauphinoise for another 30–45 minutes until the top is well browned and the vegetables are tender. This is perfect with our mushroom bourguignon (see page 117).

Serves 4 | 18 calories per serving | Prep: 10 minutes

QUICK CUCUMBER SALAD

1 cucumber

2 tbsp brown rice vinegar

½ tsp sugar

½ tsp sesame seeds

sea salt

Top and tail the cucumber, then cut it in half lengthways and remove the seeds. Cut the cucumber into thin slices or into ribbons with a peeler.

Put the rice vinegar in a bowl and add the sugar and plenty of salt. Stir until the sugar has dissolved, then add the cucumber. Toss to combine, then sprinkle over the sesame seeds.

ROOT VEGETABLE ROSTI

1 parsnip, coarsely grated

1 medium potato,
coarsely grated

1 medium beetroot,
coarsely grated

1 sweet potato,
coarsely grated

200g celeriac,
coarsely grated

1 eating apple,
coarsely grated

1 small onion,
finely chopped

1 tsp chopped sage
(optional)

25g plain flour

1 egg

low-cal oil spray

1 tbsp olive oil (optional)

sea salt and black pepper

Preheat the oven to 200°C/180°C/Gas 6.

Bring a large saucepan of water to the boil and add the grated parsnip, potato, beetroot, sweet potato and celeriac. Boil them for just 2 minutes, then drain them thoroughly and tip them into a bowl. Add the apple and onion to the bowl, then season with salt and pepper. Sprinkle in the sage, if using, and the flour, then mix in the egg.

Spray a baking tray with low-cal oil. Arrange the vegetable mixture on the tray to make a circle of about 20cm in diameter. If you have a loose-bottomed cake tin of this size, you could use it for guidance.

Press the mixture down, making sure it is spread evenly. Drizzle with the tablespoon of olive oil, if using, otherwise spray the rosti again with low-cal oil.

Bake the rosti in the oven for about 40 minutes until it's tender in the middle and crisp and well browned on the outside.

RAINBOW VEGETABLE 'COUSCOUS'

¼ cauliflower
1 small head of broccoli
1 large carrot, cut into chunks
100g baby corn, roughly chopped
¼ red cabbage, shredded
½ red pepper
small bunch of parsley, coriander or mint, finely chopped
sea salt and black pepper

Dressing (optional)
1 tbsp olive oil
juice and zest of ½ lemon
juice of 1 orange
½ tsp ground cardamom

Divide the cauliflower and the broccoli into florets. One at a time, pulse the cauliflower, broccoli, carrot, corn and cabbage in a food processor until they resemble coarse breadcrumbs in texture. Be careful not to overprocess them as you don't want them to go mushy. Dice the red pepper as finely as possible.

Add water to a large frying pan – just enough to cover the base and no more than 100ml. Add all the vegetables and season them with salt and pepper. Cook over a medium heat, stirring regularly, until the liquid has evaporated and the vegetables look fairly dry – this should take about 5 minutes.

Allow the vegetables to cool, then fluff them up a little and stir in the herbs. If you're serving the 'couscous' with a dish with a sauce you won't need a dressing, but this is also nice served on its own as a salad.

If adding the dressing, whisk the ingredients together and season them with salt and pepper. Add to the vegetable 'couscous' and serve.

BÉCHAMEL SAUCE

600ml semi-skimmed milk
1 slice of onion
2 cloves
1 bay leaf
20g cornflour
sea salt and white pepper

Put the milk in a saucepan with the slice of onion, cloves and bay leaf. Heat until the milk is just coming up to the boil, then remove the pan from the heat and leave the milk to infuse until it's almost cold.

Strain the milk into a jug, rinse out the saucepan, then pour the milk back into the pan. Mix the cornflour with a little cold water to make a smooth, thin paste. Reheat the milk and pour in the cornflour paste. Gradually bring the sauce to the boil, stirring or whisking constantly to keep it lump free. Make sure your spoon or whisk gets into all the edges, as cornflour can thicken suddenly when left alone and lumps will form.

When the sauce is the consistency of double cream, season it with salt and white pepper and it's ready to go. You can use this as a base for parsley or cheese sauce or turn it into a velouté by using vegetable stock in place of the milk – or make it with half stock and half milk.

Serves 8 | 70 calories per serving | Prep: 5 minutes | Cooking time: 10 minutes

CRANBERRY SAUCE

300g cranberries
1 piece of thinly pared orange zest
juice of 2 large sweet oranges
75g caster sugar
50ml port

Put all the ingredients in a saucepan and simmer gently until the cranberries have softened and started to pop. Stir every so often, then very thoroughly at the end – the sauce will seem very runny, but it will really firm up when it cools.

Fish out the piece of orange zest, then transfer the sauce to a serving bowl or a jar and keep it in the fridge until needed.

TOMATO SAUCE

1 tbsp olive oil

1 large onion, finely chopped

3 garlic cloves, finely chopped

2 x 400g cans of tomatoes

200ml red wine

1 tsp dried oregano

pinch of cinnamon

sea salt and black pepper

Heat the olive oil in a large saucepan. Add the onion and cook it very gently until it's soft and translucent, stirring regularly. Add the garlic and cook for another minute or so.

Add the tomatoes and wine, together with the dried oregano and cinnamon. Pour in 100ml of water, then season with salt and pepper. Bring the sauce to the boil, then turn down the heat to a simmer and cover the pan. Cook for 30 minutes, then take the lid off the pan. The sauce can be used like this while it's quite thin, or you can cook it for longer, uncovered, until it has reduced and thickened.

The recipe can be varied – for example, swap red wine for white if you want a lighter, less robust sauce, or use thyme or rosemary in place of oregano. The pinch of cinnamon adds a hint of sweetness to offset any acidity in the tomatoes.

LAKSA PASTE

2 lemongrass stalks, white centres only

3 garlic cloves

2 shallots

10g fresh root ginger

2 Thai chillies

1 tbsp puréed galangal (optional)

1 tsp ground turmeric

Roughly chop the lemongrass stalks, garlic, shallots, root ginger and chillies.

Put them in a food processor with the galangal, if using, and the turmeric, add a little water and blitz until you have a fairly smooth paste.

ONION GRAVY

5g butter
2 large onions,
thinly sliced
10g plain flour
50ml Marsala or
white wine
550ml vegetable stock
1 tsp mushroom ketchup
salt and black pepper

Heat the butter in a large saucepan and add the onions. Add a little water, then partially cover the pan and sauté the onions for a few minutes until they have softened. Turn up the heat and remove the lid from the pan, then continue to cook, stirring regularly, until the onions have started to caramelise and are a rich brown colour.

Sprinkle in the flour and stir to combine. Add the Marsala or wine and stir until you have a thick paste. Add the stock gradually – about 100ml at a time – stirring well in between each addition, until it is all incorporated.

Season the gravy with salt and pepper and add the mushroom ketchup. Bring to the boil, then turn down the heat and simmer for about 10 minutes until slightly reduced. Keep the gravy warm until you are ready to use it – it's just right with our veggie toad in the hole (see page 108).

BASIC VEGETABLE STOCK

1 tsp olive oil

2 large onions, roughly chopped

3 large carrots, well washed, chopped

200g squash or pumpkin, unpeeled, diced

4 celery sticks, sliced

2 leeks, sliced

100ml white wine or vermouth

1 large sprig of thyme

1 large sprig of parsley

1 bay leaf

a few peppercorns

Heat the olive oil in a large saucepan. Add all the vegetables and fry them over a high heat, stirring regularly, until they're starting to brown and caramelise around the edges. This will take at least 10 minutes. Add the white wine or vermouth and boil until it has evaporated away.

Cover the veg with 2 litres of water and add the herbs and peppercorns. Bring to the boil, then turn the heat down to a gentle simmer. Cook the stock, uncovered, for about an hour, stirring every so often.

Check the stock – the colour should have some depth to it. Strain it through a colander or a sieve lined with muslin, kitchen paper or coffee filter paper into a bowl and store it in the fridge for up to a week. Alternatively, pour the stock into freezer-proof containers and freeze.

Makes about 1.5 litres | Prep: 10 minutes | Cooking time: about 1 hour and 20 minutes

MUSHROOM STOCK

ingredients as for basic stock, plus:

100g mushrooms, thinly sliced

2 garlic cloves, sliced

1 tbsp tomato purée

1 tsp mushroom ketchup

Make the stock as for the basic recipe above, but add the mushrooms and sliced garlic at the beginning. Once the vegetables are well browned, add the tomato purée and mushroom ketchup. Stir them into the vegetables, then proceed as above. To make a stronger, earthier stock, soak 15g of dried mushrooms in water and add these and the soaking liquid with the water.

SPRING VEGETABLE STOCK

2 large onions,
roughly chopped

3 large carrots, well
washed, chopped

1 fennel bulb, roughly
chopped

4 celery sticks, sliced

2 leeks, sliced

pea pods

asparagus trimmings

100ml white wine
or vermouth

1 large sprig of tarragon

1 large sprig of parsley

1 bay leaf

a few peppercorns

Put all the vegetables in a large saucepan, add the white wine or vermouth and boil until the alcohol has evaporated away.

Cover the vegetables with 2 litres of water and add the herbs and peppercorns. Bring the water to the boil, then turn the heat down to a gentle simmer. Cook the stock, uncovered, for 20 minutes, stirring every so often. It's nice to keep the fresh green colour so don't cook it for longer.

Strain the stock through a colander or a sieve lined with muslin, kitchen paper or coffee filter paper into a bowl and store in the fridge for up to a week. Alternatively, pour the stock into freezer-proof containers and freeze.

POTATO BREAD BURGER BUNS

375g floury potatoes
7g sachet of
fast-acting yeast
1 tsp sugar
1 tsp salt
75ml semi-skimmed milk
1 egg
300g strong white flour,
plus extra for dusting

First make some mash. Peel the potatoes and cut them into chunks of about 3cm. Put them in a large saucepan, cover them with cold water and bring them to the boil. Cook for 10–15 minutes or until very tender. Drain the potatoes in a colander, tip them back into the saucepan and leave them to dry out for a while – the drier they are the better. Mash the potatoes until smooth – don't add any butter or milk. Leave the mash to cool to room temperature.

Put the mash in a large bowl and sprinkle over the yeast and sugar. Mix briefly so the yeast isn't all on the surface of the potato, then add the salt. Warm the milk to blood temperature, then whisk it with the egg in a bowl. Gradually mix this into the potato, then mix in the flour until you have a fairly tacky dough.

Turn the dough out on to a floured work surface and knead for a few minutes until it's soft and pliable. Put the dough back in the bowl, cover it with a damp tea towel and leave it somewhere warm to rise for about an hour.

When the dough has doubled in size, knock it back, turn it out on to the work surface again and cut it into 8 equal-sized pieces. Knead these separately and form them into rounds. Place them on a baking tray, fairly well spaced apart, then cover again and leave to rise for half an hour. Preheat the oven to 200°C/Fan 180°C/Gas 6.

After half an hour, the buns should have risen well. Put them in the oven and bake for 15–20 minutes, until they are lightly golden and sound hollow when tapped on the bottom.

Turn the buns out on to a rack and cover them with a tea towel to stop the crust firming up too much. These are great with the burgers on page 110.

POTATO PASTRY

275g floury potatoes,
preferably Maris Pipers
or King Edwards
40g chilled butter, diced
80g plain flour
1–2 tbsp semi-
skimmed milk
pinch of salt

This pastry is delicious and lower in calories than ordinary pastry made with all flour.

First make some mash. Peel the potatoes and cut them into chunks of about 3cm. Put them in a large saucepan, cover with cold water and bring to the boil. Cook for 10–15 minutes or until very tender. Drain the potatoes in a colander, tip them back into the saucepan and leave them to dry out for a while – the drier they are the better. Mash until smooth – don't add any butter or milk – and leave to cool.

To make the pastry, rub the butter into the flour in a bowl, then add 200g of cooled mash and a tablespoon of the milk. Season with a pinch of salt. Work everything together into a dough, handling it as lightly as possible. If it's too dry, add a touch more milk, but only a teaspoon at a time.

When you have a smooth dough, roll it into a ball, cover it with cling film and chill for at least half an hour before using.

A VEGGIE WEEK

Whether you're planning to go completely vegetarian or just aiming to have some meat-free days, you might like to try a week's worth of veggie eating. Here are some ideas to get you started. Feel free to swap the suggestions for lunch and evening or change to different dishes, but try to keep to the rough calorie count. If you don't have time to cook every day, you might prefer to make a big batch of soup or salad at the start of the week and enjoy it for several days – it's up to you. These menus give you about 1400 calories a day, but you can drop the snacks to take the daily total down to about 1200 if you like. Drink plenty of water and have tea and coffee with semi-skimmed milk. Always check with your doctor before going on a diet.

	BREAKFAST	LUNCH	EVENING MEAL	SNACKS
MONDAY	3 tbsp (50g) of sugar-free muesli + small pot of low-fat yoghurt Handful of berries	Buddha bowls (p.152) Small banana	Paneer and pea curry (p.124) + 50g (raw weight) brown basmati rice	Roast chickpeas (p.43) Lil's roast vegetable dip (p.44) + small wholemeal pitta + raw veg sticks
TUESDAY	1 Spiced apple muffin (p. 171) + small pot of low-fat yoghurt	Mediterranean biker brunch (p.23) + wholemeal roll (50g) 1 orange	Meatless meatballs (p.104) + 50g (raw weight) spaghetti	2 oatcakes with 2 tsp peanut butter Pear
WEDNESDAY	Small glass (150ml) fruit juice 1 slice wholemeal toast + 1 large egg, poached	Red lentil and harissa soup (p.63) + small wholemeal roll (50g) Fresh fruit salad	Latin American shepherd's pie (p.118) + broccoli	Lil's roast vegetable dip (p.44) + small wholemeal pitta + raw veg sticks 15g almonds
THURSDAY	Porridge made with 45g oats + 200ml semi-skimmed milk + water, topped with sliced banana and 1 tsp chopped almonds	Smoked tofu, avocado and spinach salad (p.70) Small pot of low-fat yoghurt	Mushroom and lentil ragu (see p.101) + green salad	Roast chickpeas (p.43) 2 oatcakes with 2 tsp peanut butter
FRIDAY	Banana and peanut smoothie – made from 250ml semi-skimmed milk + 1 chopped banana + 1 tbsp peanut butter + 1 tbsp oats	Noodle salad (p.81) Fresh fruit salad	Veggie burgers (p.110) Strawberry and orange salad (p.164)	Small bag popcorn (20g) 2 oatcakes with 2 heaped tsp reduced-fat hummus
SATURDAY	Pumpkin pancakes with apple compote (p.24) + 100ml 2%-fat Greek yoghurt	Vegetarian pasties (p.85) + green salad	Barley risotto with greens (p.139) Chocolate beetroot cake (p.162)	2 heaped tbsp reduced-fat hummus + vegetable crudites Fruit salad
SUNDAY	Avocado on toast (p.19)	Falafel (p.88)	Mushroom, leek and chestnut pie (p.98) + sugar snap peas Instant banana ice cream (p.157)	Artichoke and lemon dip (p.40) + vegetable crudites Low-fat yoghurt

And don't miss the fantastic recipes in our
other Hairy Dieters books!!

INDEX

THANKS TO YOU ALL

First of all, we want to thank Catherine Phipps for her amazing creativity and knowledge of food – you are incredible; Andrew Hayes-Watkins, our photographer, for making the food look stunning and not doing a bad job with us either. Big thanks to Lisa Harrison and Anna Burges-Lumsden, our food stylists, and Lou Kenney, their assistant. Your work is so instrumental in making this a beautiful book. Thank you to Sarah Birks for the beautiful props, and to Bev Pond-Jones and Elin Evans – you know why we love you dearly.

Abi Hartshorne is one of the most enthusiastic, knowledgeable and caring designers we've had the pleasure to work with. Jinny Johnson, our editor at large, is a powerhouse of creative prose who pilots the books through some very stormy skies. We'd also like to thank Fiona Hunter, our nutritionist, who provides us with so much good advice, and Elise See-Tai and Vicki Robinson for sterling work on proofreading and indexing.

Amanda Harris, our publisher, champion and great friend, never ceases to amaze us and it has been our privilege to work with her over the years. We know we will continue to have many adventures with her and creative director Lucie Stericker, who is simply awesome.

To Rowan Lawton and Eugenie Furniss, our literary agents, who are just flippin' marvellous. We enormously appreciate the advice you give us and the work you do on our behalf. And to our management team – Natalie Zietcer, Holly Pye, Sarah Hart, Lizzie Barroll Brown and Emma Rigarlsford – thanks for your constant enthusiasm, care and understanding.